Global democracy

To my wife Anita, our children, Sara, Lina, Josef, Olga, Joakim and Marja, and our grandchildren, Ida and Moa, in the hope that they will come to experience, and take an active part in, a well-ordered system of global democracy.

Global democracy
The case for a world government

TORBJÖRN TÄNNSJÖ

EDINBURGH UNIVERSITY PRESS

© Torbjörn Tännsjö, 2008

Edinburgh University Press Ltd
22 George Square, Edinburgh

Typeset in Linotype Palatino
by Koinonia, Manchester, and
printed and bound in Great Britain
by Cromwell Press, Trowbridge, Wilts

A CIP record for this book is available from the British Library

ISBN 978 0 7486 3498 9 (hardback)
ISBN 978 0 7486 3499 6 (paperback)

The right of Torbjörn Tännsjö to be identified as author
of this work has been asserted in accordance with
the Copyright, Designs and Patents Act 1988.

Contents

Acknowledgements

This is an entirely new book, with no parts having been published previously. I do, however, draw on earlier work, including my book on democracy and socialism (in Swedish), *Demokrati och proletär revolution* (*Democracy and Proletarian Revolution*, 1977) and another work on democracy, *Populist Democracy*, published in 1992.

Now, for a third time in my life, I have had the opportunity to examine the problems inherent in democratic theory again; this time in relation to a research project, 'Democracy Unbound', led by Professor Folke Tersman and supported by the Swedish Research Council. It has been a pleasure to work on this project and to discuss papers with the participants at various workshops. The book has grown out of a short paper on global democracy, 'Cosmopolitan Democracy Revisited', which I wrote at an early stage for 'Democracy Unbound', and later published in *Public Affairs Quarterly*, 2006. The main thrust of the argument presented here is the same as in that article, although many of the claims made in a rather dogmatic spirit in the article have here been given a much more careful defence.

I thank the Swedish Research Council for supporting the project and all the participants in the project for their valuable comments, including Gustaf Arrhenius, Lars Bergström, Girt Dimdins, Magnus Jiborn, Thomas Kaiserfeld, Henry Montgomery, Joakim Nergelius, Anna Petrén, May Thorseth, Folke Tersman and Ola Zetterquist.

Furthermore, I would like to thank Bob Goodin, Gillian Brock, Carol Gould and Carol Pateman who have kindly given good advice at various workshops, and Kai Nielsen who has made comments in correspondence. I also thank Brian Barry for giving helpful comments on an early version of the manuscript.

Finally, I thank two anonymous reviewers for Edinburgh University Press for their critical comments and helpful suggestions, Lyn Flight for the excellent and, sadly, very much needed copy editing of the book and Moyra Forrest for careful compilation of the index.

Preface

Following both the First and Second World a discussion was initiated about the best way to obviate war in the future. Some thinkers urged that we should establish a world government: H. G. Wells made this claim after the First World War,[1] while another thinker, the philosopher A. C. Ewing, made the same proposal after the Second World War, adding that the proposed world government should be democratic. There was also public support for the idea. The Broadway actor and Korean War pilot, Gary Davies, who established an organisation of citizens of the world, launched one of the most spectacular global political movements in the aftermath of the Second World War. In his own description of how he started the organisation he states:

> in May 1948 I renounced my US nationality at the Embassy in Paris, publicly declaring myself 'Citizen of the World'. With no national documents, I was considered stateless by France and ordered to leave by 12 September or be detained in jail. Meanwhile, however, the United Nations was preparing its 1948 session in Paris at the Palais de Chaillot which was, for the occasion, declared an 'international territory'. Unable to enter another country I 'entered' the new 'international territory' on the morning of 12 September and claimed 'global political asylum'. Many people got to hear of this through the international media and gave their support. A council of international intellectuals was formed, led by Albert Camus.[2]

Once you became a member of the organisation, you were to request a World Citizen's passport from the headquarters of the organisation and its 'International Registry of World Citizens', and then burn your national passport.

Less radical, but probably more influential, was the World

Federalist Movement (WFM), a global citizens movement with member and associated organisations around the world, founded in 1947 in Montreux and with its headquarters in New York.

However, neither philosophical arguments nor global movements succeeded in convincing the world that the time was ripe for a world government, let alone for global democracy. Probably it was not. Nevertheless, in both cases in the aftermath of each world war, the discussion propelled politicians towards considerable and remarkable results: the establishment of the League of Nations and the United Nations.

Now that the Cold War is long over, and we can see new trends of globalisation around the world, discussion about the global political order is once again gaining momentum. Moreover, it is not only problems concerning war and peace that are now fuelling the debate, but topics such as a concern for global justice and a vital interest in a sustainable environment have been added to the original rationale for global democracy. We have seen initiatives such as those intended to sway opinion towards a global peoples' assembly at the United Nations.[3] Former United Nations Secretary-General Boutros Boutros-Ghali is among those leading politicians supporting such initiatives:

> If the process of democratization does not move forward at the international level, democracy at the level of the nation-state will also diminish ... In the process of globalization, problems which can only be solved effectively at the global level, are multiplying and requirements of political governance are extending beyond state borders accordingly. Increased decision-making at the global level therefore is inevitable ... We need to promote the democratization of globalization, before globalization destroys the foundations of national and international democracy.[4]

According to Boutros-Ghali, the establishment of a parliamentary assembly at the United Nations 'has become an indispensable step to achieve democratic control of globalization'.[5] The number of books and articles urging global governance as an answer to global problems is legion, including David Held, *The Global Covenant* (2002);

Preface

Kwame Appiah, *Cosmopolitanism* (2006); Thomas Pogge, *World Poverty and Human Rights* (2002); David McNally, *Another World Is Possible* (2002); Neil Smith, *The Endgame of Globalization* (2005); Kai Nielsen, *Globalization and Justice* (2003); and Peter Singer, *One World* (2002). And this new discussion is taking place in a situation where the time *is* ripe for global democracy.

It should be noted that my claim that the time is ripe for *global democracy* is more radical than the claims usually made in the recent debate even by so-called cosmopolitans. However, this more radical claim can be substantiated by solid arguments, or so I will attempt to show.

In my early youth I became a member of Gary Davies' Citizens of the World, which was still influential in the late 1960s, but my real theoretical interest in global matters was raised twenty years later, in the late 1980s. This was just before the collapse of the Soviet Union and Gorbachev was still in power when my first book on the topic was conceived. It had dawned upon me that global matters raise particular problems to do with democratic theory. In my book, *Populist Democracy: A Defence* (1992), I devoted a part to the problem of global democracy, and I defended the possibility and desirability of global democracy.

But how should global democracy be established? I argued that we should build on the United Nations which should be democratised. I still think this argument was correct; however, I also argued that the first step towards global democracy should be to establish *regional* political unions such as the European Union. I now believe this view to be mistaken. In order to see this, consider the following questions: how could such unions be persuaded to overcome their rivalry and unite into one global democracy?; how could they be convinced to give up their sovereignty while facing a constant threat from one another?; how could they be convinced to grant a monopoly on the use of force to the United Nations?

I had no serious answer to questions such as these, and I think perhaps I tended not to think seriously about the problem. Of course, if there are many competing super powers in the world, then these super powers will be hard put to give up their monopoly on the use of force. Some people seem not yet to have seen this problem.

xi

I think of philosophers such as Habermas and Derrida, who have supported a militarily strong Europe as a balancing factor in world politics to the USA. But this means indefinite competition, rivalry and a virtual state of war.

Something has changed radically since I wrote my book in the late 1980s, however. We now live in a world where there exists only one unique superpower: the United States. This is an often-lamented fact, but those who find it problematic ought to reconsider their position. Rather than being an obstacle to the establishment of global democracy, the existence of one sole superpower is a necessary prerequisite for it. At least this is what I argue in the present book. If I am right about this, then this means that, not only is this a propitious time for global democracy, we are experiencing a unique opportunity for achieving it. The window of opportunity, moreover, may be a narrow one, so we should seize the moment.

Initiatives such as the Global Peoples' Assembly are very promising. However, they will have no effect unless they gain strong support from a global political movement committed to the cause of creating a democratic world order. Will they get the necessary support? Since the moral and intellectual case for global democracy is strong, as I will try to show in this book, since the time is ripe for global democracy, and since the window of opportunity may be narrow there is every reason to believe that soon the necessary support for global democracy will indeed be forthcoming.

Many young people today live and feel like world citizens. They use new media to communicate. They walk the entire globe and they socialise across national borders. They feel the need for global action, for example, when it comes to problems to do with war, human rights, global injustices and global warming, yet they lack a clear political goal. Such a goal does exist, however; they need only come to see this. It is not too far-fetched to assume that many of them will come to do so, that is, come to *act* politically as world citizens, once they realise that global democracy is a necessity – if we want to come to grips with urgent global problems – that it is feasible and, most importantly, many influential thinkers to the contrary notwithstanding, that it is desirable in its own right.

1
The problem

1. Introduction

Today when we consider global problems and the prospects for a world government we tend to think mainly about the present and the recent past, including the last century. However, since at least the seventeenth century there have been some voices advocating 'cosmopolitanism', in a strong sense implying the necessity for a world government.[1] During the twentieth century some thinkers who have espoused a belief in world government have added that it should be democratic; they have argued that the world population should elect the world parliament directly and the world parliament should select a world government.[2]

The rationale behind the first of these claims, the claim that a world government is needed, has been the idea that there are many problems facing humanity which seem to be intractable if tackled on a less than global level. We need, therefore, a world government. The first and foremost of these problems is, of course, how to obtain a secure and lasting peace in the world. The idea is that just as peace has been secured in a certain territory once a state has been established there, then peace would be secured in the world once a world government with a monopoly on military forces has been established. Other problems have, however, been added in recent times to this traditional rationale in the discussion about

Global democracy

world government. Now we find additional problems to do with the environment (global warming), crimes against humanity, corruption (as I was reminded by South African philosophers when giving a talk there on this subject) and global justice. Yet those who have advocated a world government have been in the minority, and their proposals have been met with scepticism. A standard objection has been that the idea of a world government is utopian (raised already by Rousseau). Moreover, many believe that, even if a world government could be established, this would not be desirable. There are better options available to humanity. So many attempts have been made to find solutions to global problems not involving any cosmopolitan government. Some thinkers have gone to considerable lengths to find methods of approaching global justice and perpetual peace without resorting to world government. We encounter here a Kantian tradition, emanating from Immanuel Kant himself and continuing with Hans Kelsen and John Rawls in the twentieth century, arguing that the prospect of a world government should be perceived as something to be feared, rather than something valuable in its own right.

So the establishment of a world government is not an obvious solution to the global problems facing humanity. As a matter of fact, there seem to exist, not just two, but three radically different approaches to the traditional problem of peace and the emerging problems to do with the environment, international justice, corruption and so forth. They are as follows.

The first of these approaches is the idea that these problems *are* best handled through the establishment of a world government. I will speak of this putative solution as a world 'federation', but observe that there are many other possible uses of the word 'federation'.

Another idea has been that we should reform each nation-state; if we do, then it would be possible through peaceful negotiation between sovereign nation-states to find solutions to the problems facing humanity. I will speak here of an anarchistic position since the position means that the existing anarchic world order should be respected, while global problems are handled through voluntary

2

and temporary agreements between independent nation-states. It was the opinion, not only of the well-known deontological moral philosopher Immanuel Kant that such a solution should be sought, but also of his equally well-known main (utilitarian) rival in moral philosophy, Jeremy Bentham: they both believed that if each and every one of the states themselves were internally reformed in certain ways, an anarchic system of peaceful cooperation between independent states would evolve.

Even if Bentham was certainly more optimistic about the near future than Kant, these authors agreed in their respective *A Plan for an Universal and Perpetual Peace* and *Perpetual Peace* that independent and sovereign nation-states can learn to live peacefully together if some domestic conditions are met; that is, no colonies, no secret diplomacy, and a free press, according to Bentham, and a republican political system, according to Kant.

Note, however, that this adherence to what I have called an anarchistic position did not stop Kant from advocating a 'federation of free states', a contradiction in terms, according to my use of the word 'federation'. What Kant referred to, however, was the mere possibility that free and independent states voluntary made international binding *agreements* between themselves.

There is also a third compromise position. We should seek to establish a kind of hybrid between an anarchistic and federal solution, where some decisions are taken on a global level, while other decisions are taken on a national, international or regional level, where it is possible, for example, to have part of the population of two states deciding about some matters of common concern. This hybrid position is taken up in the recent discussion by many of those who are usually described as advocates of global or cosmopolitan democracy.

I will reject both the anarchic solution suggested by Kant and Bentham and the hybrid position (including the idea that different decisions could be taken by various different transnational bodies) advocated by many contemporary 'cosmopolitan' writers. As a matter of fact, I will try to show that *these* putative alternatives to the establishment of a sovereign world government are indeed utopian.

The compromise position is not stable. Even if it could be established, it would not last for long. I will also argue that the problem with the idea of respecting the existing anarchic state, searching for solutions to global problems though voluntary agreements between independent nation-states is that such agreements cannot be found with respect to many pressing global problems facing humanity. Furthermore, even when solutions can be found, these will be temporary and unstable unless a world government is established. In a way, Immanuel Kant himself admits this, as we will see when he speaks of his desired order as inherently a 'state of war', and yet he prefers it to a world government.

All this means that, if we go for any one of these alternative putative solutions, we have to make large sacrifices in terms of a lack of peace, justice and a good environment. But even if it can be shown that we need a world government in order to solve important global problems, such a world government could take various different forms. Are there any reasons to believe that the most efficient kind of world government would be democratic? Remember that some advocates of a world government have opted for various elitist solutions, such as those advocated by H. G. Wells.

Once I have shown that we need a world government in the first place, I will attempt to show that such a government should take a democratic form. I will argue that, not only is a democratic world government an effective instrument when it comes to the solution of pressing global problems, but also that *only* a democratic world government is a feasible and realistic political goal. So unless we establish a democratic world government it is unlikely that we will establish any world government at all. The solution to pressing global problems, then, *is* global democracy.

The defence of a *democratic* world government goes some way towards meeting the caveat put forward by Immanuel Kant that a world government is not desirable as such. What he feared was global tyranny, and it is true almost by definition that a democratic government is not tyrannical. However, even a democratic world government could be conceived of as degenerating into tyranny, of being at variance with the demands of human nature, our cultural and economic needs and so forth. Chapter 7 is, therefore, devoted to the question of whether it might be worth the price in terms of perpetual war, global injustices and environmental problems to keep a system of independent national-states in place. I will try to show that, in the final analysis, there are no good reasons to fear a global democracy any more than there are good reasons to fear democracy on the national level.

2. The structure of the argument

In Chapters 2 to 4 I will discuss the most important arguments, that is, those arising from peace, global justice and the environment in defence of the necessity for a world government. I will conclude that, unless we resort to world government, we will obtain neither global peace, justice nor a good environment. Moreover, I will argue that a world government is capable of handling these problems. So the strong claim is that a world government is both necessary and sufficient if we want to handle these problems in a satisfactory manner.

Of course, the most difficult position to defend is that a world government is necessary at all. Once it is in place, being sovereign and in command of resources on a global scale, it is not far-fetched to assume that it could deal with the problems with which it is faced. At least this is so if this claim is understood with some caution. Of course, there is no *guarantee* that some unexpected disaster will not strike our planet at some time during the next few hundred years. If the Earth is hit by a comet and blown to pieces, there is little a world government could do about it. Although if the event is predictable, there may be something that can be done, time to avert the threat, or possibly establish a settlement on another planet. In such an unlikely event, it would be helpful to have a world government commanding global resources for the enterprise. However, in the *very* long run I suppose we have to acknowledge that there will be no life either on Earth or in our galactic vicinity. So my claim that a world government is sufficient should be understood in relation to the *type* of problems I discuss in this book to do with war, global justice and the environment – as we know them. Moreover, in order to be sufficient to the solution of these problems, the world government must take the right form.

In Chapter 5, assuming that a world government is both necessary and sufficient if we want to solve some of the most pressing problems facing humanity, I discuss in what form it is sufficient. I discuss whether it can, and should, be democratic. I argue that, in order to fulfil its purpose, it must be democratic.

Now, there are many competing conceptions of democracy, and I will discuss in some detail what particular concept is applicable in the present context. My conjecture will be that only a radical and 'populist' version of democracy stands a chance of commanding the required public support in order to become a reality. I will also argue that a populist democracy (of a form to be explained) is likely to provide an efficient form of world government – where the efficiency is judged in relation to the goals it is supposed to fulfil: to achieve global peace, global justice and a sustainable environment.

In Chapter 6 I give a detailed account of how we can initiate a political process which stands a chance of culminating in the establishment of a global democracy. I aim to show that this type of policy is, in an important sense of the word, 'realistic'. I draw a 'road map' to global democracy.

A crucial assumption in the discussion is the fact that, for the moment, there exists only one real super power in the world, the USA, and contrary to what has often been assumed, is a very *favourable* condition to the establishment of a world government. As a matter of fact, I will argue, that for this very reason we are facing, historically speaking, a unique possibility – a narrow window of opportunity – of sorting out the most pressing global problems facing humanity.

Having argued that global democracy is a *sine qua non* if we want to solve some crucial problems facing humanity, and after having argued that this project is, in an important sense of the word, 'realistic', in particular if we can seize the opportunity created by the fact that, for the time being, only one super power exists, I raise the question in Chapter 7 of whether a global democracy is really, as such, desirable.

The problem

Here I examine the most important arguments to the effect that it is not desirable. These are mainly the communitarian argument arising from the idea that there is no genuine global cultural community in the world on which to build, the related economist argument that there is no genuine global economic community to build from, the argument that a hybrid solution would be better than an outright federate one and, finally, the argument based on a fear that a global democracy might turn out to be a tyranny of the majority over many important minorities. If these arguments were correct, then we would be in deep trouble. We would then have to accept that, although there is a solution to the problems facing humanity, we should not take advantage of it.

However, having examined the most important arguments to the effect that a world government is not desirable, even if it takes a radically democratic shape; having also in this chapter repudiated the compromise idea that a hybrid should be established, where sovereignty is divided between different political bodies, rather than an outright global democracy with one sovereign world parliament, I conclude that, not only is a global democracy a *sine qua non* if we want to solve pressing problems facing humanity, it is as such highly desirable.

Finally in Chapter 8 I review the most important results in this book.

2
The argument arising from peace

1. *The main arguments*

There are many arguments that have been thought by some to lead us to the conclusion that what is needed in today's world is a sovereign world government. I will not go into all such putative arguments but focus on those that I think are the most promising: that is, those arising from peace; justice; and the environment. The general line of reasoning is that there are global problems concerning war, injustices and the environment that can be dealt with satisfactorily only if a sovereign world government is established.

Even if all these arguments are successful, this does not mean that a sovereign world government is in the final analysis desirable. There may be some problems with such a government that are so serious that we would prefer to live with wars, injustices, human rights violations and environmental problems rather than establish it. However, even if only one of these arguments succeeds, the result is that if we do not see a world government as desirable as such, we have to make a very serious and rather tragic choice: we have then to bear with these problems. So the discussion of these arguments should be of interest both to those who welcome and those who fear the very idea of a world government.

As a matter of fact, I believe that, at least to some extent, all the arguments succeed. I concede that perhaps there is a way of achieving global peace without resorting to world government, but this road to global peace seems far from safe; it is certainly much slower than the one that proceeds via the establishment of a world government, and the result may eventually be overturned when new relationships between independent nation-states evolve. Moreover, the establishment of a world government, and even the first steps towards its establishment, as they will be described when I sketch a road map to global democracy, are likely to strengthen those aspects of global development that engender more peaceful conditions. In particular, it is likely to promote the establishment of democracy around the world, and democracy, at least when it is firmly established, tends to lead to peace. It is safe to conclude that, without democracy, perpetual peace is not possible.

It is probable that we must resort to the establishment of a world government if we want to establish global justice. I will defend this claim in the next chapter. It might be the case that, just as the establishment of democracy in all countries would promote global peace, the establishment of some kind of socialism in all countries would promote global justice. However, even if this is the case, it would not be a good idea to put the problem of global injustices to one side while waiting for socialism to prevail. We need action now, and the kind of action that is needed, in order to counter the most glaring global injustices, seems to presuppose the existence of a world government. I will argue that these injustices cannot be obviated altogether, if we do not resort to socialism, but they can be very much reduced once a world government is in place.

Finally, it is *obvious*, it seems to me, that some of the environmental problems facing humanity cannot be resolved, not even in the long term, unless a world government is established. Here the problem of global warming is what first comes to mind to the contemporary reader, but there are other pressing environmental problems as well. Neither democracy nor socialism, or even both in combination, in the individual countries of the world is sufficient to deal with some of the problems with which we are now faced, and which will possibly face us in the future. This is what I will try to establish in Chapter 4.

So, if my arguments in the first three chapters of this book are on the right track, then we do seriously have to ponder the question of whether a global democracy can be established. Moreover, if it can be instituted, we must evaluate it not only as a means of solving some pressing global problems, but also on its own merits. Would it be a good thing or not to live in a world governed by a world government?

For the moment, however, I restrict my argument to the claim that a world government is both necessary and sufficient if we want to solve pressing global problems. Now to the arguments in defence of this more restricted claim.

The argument to be examined in the present chapter is that emanating from peace. The arguments from justice and the environment are discussed in the following chapters.

2. The argument arising from peace

One argument in defence of world government is very simple. Unless a world government is established, there will be war in the world. If a world government is established, peace will be guaranteed. Surely, therefore, as we do not want war, so we ought to opt for a world government.

The idea behind this reasoning is an analogy with how peace has been guaranteed within nation-states. A national monopoly in the hands of one sovereign national government on the use of violence has been established, and this monopoly on violence in the nation-state has safeguarded peace within it. The same, therefore, should be attempted at a global level, with the world government holding a monopoly on the use of violence throughout the world.

Is this analogy a good one? No, it is not, it has sometimes been claimed, as nation-states have typically been established in a forceful and highly violent manner, and certainly, we do not want to establish a world government in that manner. This is how Hans Kelsen put the point in 1944:

The suggestion to secure international peace through a World

State is based on the analogy assumed to exist between a
World State and the national State by which national peace is
so effectively secured. This analogy, however, seems to be not
very favorable to the intentions of those who wish to bring
about the peace of the world by methods which comply with
the principles of democracy: liberty and equality, applied to
international relations. For the national State with its effect of
national peace is not the result of an agreement voluntarily
negotiated by free and equal individuals. The supposition
maintained by the natural law doctrine ... has been abandoned
and replaced by another hypothesis according to which the State
comes into existence through hostile conflicts between social
groups of different economic structure. In the course of these
armed conflicts, which have the character of bloody wars, the
most aggressive and warlike group subjugates the others and
imposes upon them a peace order.[1]

One possible reaction to this would be to bite the bullet and argue
that world government *is* a necessity and that, if necessary, it should
be established in a forceful manner. Bertrand Russell famously and
somewhat desperately took this stance once,[2] and claimed that the
use, or at least the serious threat of use, of nuclear weapons could be
helpful to the cosmopolitan cause, although he later came to regret
it. Indeed, there were good grounds for regret. It is neither desirable nor possible, at least not in the present historical situation, to
establish a world government through the use of force. For reasons
to be spelled out in the following chapters, however, I hold a more
optimistic view of the *possibility* of establishing a world government
today without resort to force. Kelsen's view is now dated. We should
remember that in the past there have existed systems that come
close to world government: the Roman Empire is the best example
of this (mentioned by Kelsen), although this was indeed established
in a forceful manner. Once in place, however, its origin could not
reasonably be evoked as an argument for its abolishment, and at the
present time we are experiencing an international situation, never
thought of by Kelsen, where a peaceful transition to world govern-

ment is feasible. This is where the United States enters the picture. Since the collapse of the Soviet Union the United States has been the sole and unique world superpower, and this will remain a fact for the foreseeable future. We should not complain about this fact but, rather, take advantage of it. Not since the height of the Roman Empire have the circumstances been so favourable to the idea of a world government as they are today. Moreover, contrary to the situation some 2,000 years ago, the idea of a global *democracy* has become a viable option, and for the first time a *peaceful* road towards global democracy lies open before us. Russell's speculations about the use of nuclear weapons to create a world government are now happily redundant.

But is a world government necessary if we want to guarantee global peace? Is it sufficient? Both these questions need to be addressed.

3. Can we have peace without global democracy?
Kant and Bentham

Immanuel Kant cautiously defended the idea that we can have peace without a world government. According to Kant, the establishment of republican governments would mean the first step towards perpetual peace. The second step would be the establishment of international law, a league of nations, settling disputes between independent nation-states. However, he does not take for granted that his idea will work. This is how he formulates his question:

> The sole established constitution that follows from the idea [Idee] of an original contract, the one on which all of a nation's just [rechtliche] legislation must be based, is republican. For, first, it accords with the principles of the *freedom* of the members of a society (as men), second, it accords with the principles of the *dependence* of everyone on a single, common [source of] legislation (as subjects), and third, it accords with the law of the equality of them all (as citizens). Thus, so far as [the matter of] right is concerned, republicanism is the original foundation of

all forms of civil constitution. Thus, the one question remaining
is this; does it also provide the only foundation for perpetual
peace?[3]

Now, the solution to the problem of how to obtain perpetual peace,
according to Kant, is the establishment of a league of republican
nations. This league must not violate the sovereignty of the nation-
states:

> This league does not seek any power of the sort possessed by
> nations, but only the maintenance and security of each nation's
> own freedom, as well as that of the other nations leagued with it,
> without their having thereby to subject themselves to civil laws
> and their constraints (as men in the state of nature must do).[4]

Kant does concede that a world republic may in principle be a means
– and even the best means – to perpetual peace. However, as we will
see, he doesn't like the idea of a world republic (his arguments to
this effect will be discussed in Chapter 7), which he believes to be
undesirable. So, in its place we must resort to the kind of solution
he advocates, where sovereign states, in a league of nations, voluntarily agree to keep peace with one another. This is how he touches
upon the idea of a world republic but dismisses it:

> Reason can provide related nations with no other means for
> emerging from the state of lawlessness, which consists solely of
> war, than that they give up their savage (lawless) freedom, just
> as individual persons do, and, by accommodating themselves
> to the constraints of common law, establish a *nation of peoples*
> (*civitas genitum*) that (continually growing) will finally include
> all the people on the earth. But they do not will to do this because
> it does not conform to their idea of the right of nations, and
> consequently they discard in *hypothesis* what is true in *thesis*.
> So (if everything is not to be lost) in place of the positive idea
> of *a world republic* they put only the *negative* surrogate of an
> enduring, ever expanding *federation* that prevents war and curbs

the tendency of that hostile inclination to defy the law, though there will always be constant danger of their breaking loose.[5]

However, if we forgo in *hypothesis* what is true in *thesis* and do not establish a world government, is there any reason to believe that a peaceful order can be obtained?

Here Kant makes an interesting reference to the self-interest of the rulers. Kant writes like a contemporary 'public choice' scholar, who wants to explain social facts with reference exclusively to the consequences of the rational actions of egoistic agents:

> the republican constitution also provides for this desirable result, namely, perpetual peace, and the reason for this is as follows: If ... the consent of the citizenry is required in order to determine whether or not there will be war, it is natural that they consider all its calamities before committing themselves to so risky a game ... By contrast, under a nonrepublican constitution, where subjects are not citizens, the easiest thing in the world to do is to declare war. Here the ruler is not a fellow citizen, but the nation's owner, and war does not affect his table, his hunt, his places of pleasure, his court festivals, and so on. Thus, he can decide to go to war for the most meaningless of reasons, as if it were a kind of pleasure party, and he can blithely leave its justification ... to his diplomatic corps, who are always prepared for such exercises.[6]

We have seen that, even if in theory (or, 'in thesis'), according to Kant, a world republic would be the best means for achieving perpetual peace, we must be satisfied with a league of sovereign nations agreeing to peaceful relations between one another. He seems to believe that, in the very long term, such a league may come to be established, but, we should bear in mind, he is not too optimistic in this respect. Even if it is eventually established, and if there are no more wars, 'there will always be constant danger of their breaking loose'. When new power relations between the free republican states evolve, when strong states are weakened and weak states are strengthened and new coalitions are formed, then the order among them may be upset.

Jeremy Bentham was more optimistic in *his* plan for eternal peace:

> The following plan has for its basis two fundamental proposi-
> tions: 1. The reduction and fixation of the force of the several
> nations that compose the European system; 2. The emancipation
> of the distant dependencies of each state.

Then a Congress or Diet should be constituted along the following lines:

> Such a Congress or Diet might be constituted by each power
> sending two deputies to the place of meeting; one of these to be
> the principal, the other to act as an occasional substitute.
> The proceedings of such Congress or Diet should be all public.
> Its power would consist, 1. In reporting its opinion; 2. In causing
> that opinion to be circulated in the dominions of each state …
> 3. After a certain time, in putting the refractory state under the
> ban of Europe.

How should the world society deal with refractory states?

> There might, perhaps, be no harm in regulating, as a last
> resource, the contingent to be furnished by the several states
> for enforcing the decrees of the court. But the necessity for the
> employment of this resource would, in all human probability,
> be superseded for ever by having recourse to the much more
> simple and less burthensome expedient, of introducing into
> the instrument by which such court was instituted, a clause
> guaranteeing the liberty of the press in each state, in such sort,
> that the diet might find no obstacle to its giving, in every state,
> to its decrees, and to every paper whatever which it might think
> proper to sanction with its signature, the most extensive and
> unlimited circulation.

15

Obviously, the treatment of the subject of perpetual peace put forward by both Bentham and Kant is highly speculative. As these thinkers were writing at the end of the eighteenth century there was little experience of republicanism, democracy and freedom of the press. Also there was no tendency for colonial powers to give up their colonies, in fact, quite the contrary. Since then a host of wars have been fought; with the twentieth century possibly being the most violent period ever experienced by humankind.

The number of wars fought since Bentham and Kant wrote their treatises seems to be legion. Who knows how many there have been?

As a matter of fact, we do know as an exact count now exists in the form of the *Human Security Report*. This is how the situation is recapitulated in that survey:

A newly revised dataset tracks the number of wars since the Congress of Vienna ended the Napoleonic era in 1815 ... Between 1816 and 2002 there were 199 international wars (including wars of colonial conquest and liberation) and 251 civil wars – one international war on average for every 1.3 civil wars over the entire period.[7]

This is not a nice picture. If we are not impressed by these statistics, we may turn to books such as Jonathan Glover's *Humanity*, to learn more about the concrete details of the atrocities of the last century. According to Glover:

In Europe at the start of the twentieth century most people accepted the authority of morality. They thought there was a moral law, which was self-evidently to be obeyed. Immanuel Kant had written of the two things which fill the mind with admiration and awe, 'the starry heavens above me and the moral law within me'. In Cambridge in 1895, a century after Kant, Lord Acton still had no doubts: 'Opinions alter, manners change, creeds rise and fall, but the moral law is written on the tablets of eternity'. At the start of the twentieth century, reflective

Europeans were also able to believe in moral progress, and to see human viciousness and barbarism as in retreat. At the end of the century, it is hard to be confident either about the moral law or about moral progress.[8]

Is this kind of gloomy scepticism warranted? Some seem to think that it is not. They stress something that went unnoticed by Glover. We seem now to have entered a period in history where war is not as prevalent as it once was. Over at least the last fifteen years we have experienced a spectacular trend towards a more peaceful coexistence between nations. This is how this trend is depicted in the recent *Human Security Report*:

- The number of armed conflicts around the world has declined by more than 40% since the early 1990s.
- Between 1991 (the high point for the post-World War II period) and 2004, 28 armed struggles for self-determination started or restarted, while 43 were contained or ended. There were just 25 armed secessionist conflicts under way in 2004, the lowest number since 1976.
- Notwithstanding the horrors of Rwanda, Srebrenica and elsewhere, the number of genocides and politicides plummeted by 80% between the 1988 high point and 2001.
- International crises, often harbingers of war, declined by more than 70% between 1981 and 2001.
- The dollar value of major international arms transfers fell by 33% between 1990 and 2003. Global military expenditure and troop numbers declined sharply in the 1990s as well.
- The number of refugees dropped by some 45% between 1992 and 2003, as more and more wars came to an end.[9]

Should we rely on this recent trend? Does it mean that there is no need for a world government if we want to attain perpetual peace?

I think this conclusion is premature, but in order to assess it we must look more closely at the *mechanisms* that have been held to explain the recent more peaceful trend. One such mechanism is certainly the one previously mentioned by Bentham: the abolition of colonialism. The other often mentioned condition is democracy (republicanism, in Kant's words). Finally, we have the common claim made by Kant and Bentham that a league of nations, or a diet, would finally do the trick. The contemporary version of such a league of nations is, of course, the United Nations.

Let us look more closely into these three ideas about the abolition of colonies, the establishment of democracy and the forming of a league of nations to see whether they may prove sufficient for a system of perpetual peace.

4. The abolition of the colonial system

To a large extent, Bentham's claim that the colonial system should be abolished has since come true. It is not that the colonial powers peacefully came to the realisation that they should give up their colonies; in most cases they were given up only after decades of fierce warfare. These wars fought over the colonies have been one important factor explaining why there have been so many wars since the days of Bentham and Kant. But these days are over now, aren't they? The *Human Security Report* states:

> By the early 1980s the wars of liberation from colonial rule, which had accounted for 60% to 100% of all international wars fought since the early 1950s, had virtually ended. With the demise of colonialism, a major driver of warfare around the world – one that had caused 81 wars since 1816 – simply ceased to exist.[10]

Viewing what is now taking place in Iraq and in Israel/Palestine I cannot help but feel that this is a much exaggerated view of the current state of affairs. There are few nominal colonies left, but the system is still in place in a more informal manner; wars are still fought over scarce natural resources such as oil. It is true that there is only one superpower today, and this may mean that earlier superpower rivalry over such issues has evaporated, which may, in turn, generate more peaceful international relations. We see a kind of pax Americana right now, but there is no guarantee that this situation will continue in the future. On the contrary, there are good reasons to believe that, if we do not seize the moment and establish a world government new conflicts will emerge in the future.

With the probable rise of rival superpowers, we may well be thrown back into conflicts similar to those we have just left behind us. There is little reason to believe that such future conflicts will be any less brutal than the ones we know about from our recent past. If the United States, the European Union, China, Russia and India come to compete on equal terms, perhaps in the form of various new different alliances, for scarce natural resources it is highly likely that we will see a return to the only too well-known colonial ambitions of the past.

5. Democracy as a means to eternal peace

The main theory put forward by Kant was that republicanism in nation-states would prepare the road to perpetual peace. This has been picked up in contemporary discussions, but now as the idea that democracy, rather than republicanism, may engender perpetual peace. Since democracy implies republicanism, this does not make much substantial difference. Two important claims have been made in the discussion: first, that democracies do not engage one another in wars; and secondly, that democracies do not initiate wars with non-democracies, instead resorting to armed combat only as a defensive measure. Are these claims correct? If they are correct, does this mean that we can have peace without establishing a world government?

Is it true that democracies do not wage war against one another? In 1997, University of Hawaii professor, Rudy Rummel, published his seminal examination of all major international wars for the period between 1816 and 1991. While his account includes upwards of 350 dyads of nations engaged in major international conflict, he claims that not one of these pairings included two opposing democracies.[11] These data have been questioned, however. As a matter of fact, there

seem to be some *obvious* counter-examples to them. For example, the
First World War seems to be (violently) at odds with the thesis. How
does Rummel account for this? In an interview he claims:

> Then there was Imperial Germany's war against the democratic
> allies in World War I. Its citizens did have certain civil and
> political rights, including universal male suffrage, and the legis-
> lature was fully elected. But the unelected Kaiser appointed the
> chancellor, directly controlled the army and involved himself
> in foreign affairs.[12]

Note, however, that the political parties in the various European
parliaments, *including* the German Reichstag, and also including the
Social Democrats, voted for war credits (this is what caused the split
of the Social Democratic parties and what led to the emergence of
Left Socialist and eventually Communist Parties worldwide).

Another, rarely mentioned, example is the war between Finland
(clearly a democracy) and the Allies during what has euphemisti-
cally been called the 'continuation' war, where the United Kingdom
(also clearly a democracy) declared war on Finland on 6 December
1941.[13] Let us assume, however, that, even if there are exceptions,
there is *some* truth in the hypothesis. Of course, how we assess it has
much to do with not only how we define 'democracy' and 'war' but
also on how we are prepared to treat recalcitrant evidence from the
two world wars.

What then about the claim that democracies do not act aggres-
sively against non-democratic states? Adherents of the theory that
democracy is a means of avoiding war usually paint a stunningly
rosy picture. The Virginia law professor, John Norton Moore, writes,
for example, that in an examination of all major international wars
since the inception of the United Nations in 1945, only one could
reasonably be deemed international aggression on the part of
democratic states – that being the Suez War of 1956 in which Britain
and France went to war with Egypt as a reaction to the nationalisa-
tion of the Suez Canal.[14]

If this claim is true, it is good news indeed. But is it true? Again, this has much to do with how we define 'aggression'. However, unless we restrict the use of the term in a ridiculously narrow way, it is clear that the number of exceptions to this rule, if it is a rule in the first place, are numerous: take for example the role of France in Indochina and Algeria; the role of the United States in Korea and its war in Vietnam; the continued Israeli occupation of Palestine (both Israel and Palestine must qualify as democracies or is an occupied democracy a contradiction in terms?); the current American-led occupation of Iraq; and the American incursions into Latin America during the twentieth century such as Panama and Grenada.

Even if in a narrow sense of the word (where an action must incur more than one thousand combat casualties to qualify as a war), many of the American invasions in Latin America did not amount to 'war', they are real enough to count in the *present* context. How does Rummel comment on examples such as these? He does not deny that they exist, of course, but he claims, in a way that is reminiscent of Bentham, that they go against the true spirit of democracy:

> during the Cold War actions were taken about which in hindsight many democrats are embarrassed. Even then, there was no military action between democracies. Still, democracies are not monolithic; they are divided into many agencies, some of which operate in secrecy and are really totalitarian subsystems connected only at the top to democratic processes. Examples are the military, especially in wartime, and such secret services as the CIA. Outside of the democratic sunshine and processes, these islands of power can do things that would be forbidden, were they subject to democratic scrutiny. The answer to this problem is more democratic control. With the spread of democracy around the world, armies and secret services can be eliminated altogether.[15]

This may be true, yet if it is true, we are at least allowed to conclude that democracy is *consistent* with policies such as these.

Rummel furthermore claims that democracies on average behave less violently than non-democratic states:

on the average democracies have much less violence than other forms of government, and this knowledge gives us the greatest practical tool for reducing world political violence by and within countries.[16]

However, even if this is true on average (although it is difficult to say how we should calculate this kind of average), there is one *extremely* violent example where a democracy has waged war against a small country: the United States war against Vietnam (as well as Laos and Cambodia), where biological warfare and saturation bombings were resorted to, where atrocities were committed and where *millions* of people were killed. No non-democratic state achieved anything comparable during the same period. So, once again, it seems to be acceptable to conclude that democracy is *consistent* with (very) violent behaviour in wars directed at non-democratic enemies.

Where does all this leave the claim that it is possible to achieve global peace without a world government? It is obvious that this claim has not been established. The most important problems have already been indicated. However, it might be a good idea to elaborate on them somewhat.

First, the data here are 'epidemiological'. It may well be true that democracies are reluctant to go to war with one another (and the mechanism may well be, as was suggested by Kant, self-interest of the political leaders). However, this does not exclude the possibility that there is a common cause behind both peaceful behaviour of a state and the possibility of establishing democracy. Unless we believe, however, that democracy will necessarily spread around the world, we cannot rely on this mechanism. When it is time for war, democracy's time may be up.

We must also be very cautious when discussing the very recent trend towards peace, observed in the *Human Security Report*, quoted above. Such trends, as are there observed, could easily be reversed. In many ways, they seem to be the result of the existing pax Americana, which may well come to be challenged by the emergence of future competing superpowers, and coalitions of them, in the world.

Moreover, we know that some democracies do sometimes use

force to overthrow democracy in other countries. Examples abound, particularly with reference to the United States: an American backed coup in Indonesia in 1965 resulted in the massacre of approximately 700,000 people with 750,000 arrested; the United States overturned the democracies of Allende in Chile, Arbenz in Guatemala and Mossadegh in Iran; it supported the overthrow of the democratic government by a military coup in Thailand in 1976; American attempts to bring down the Sandinistas government in Nicaragua were condemned by the International Court of Justice and Equality through Law (the 'World Court'); and there have been more recent attempts to topple the democratically elected President Chavez in Venezuela.

In addition to this, we should bear in mind that democracies have periodically actively supported non-democratic governments against democratic movements. The most conspicuous example of this is, of course, the support that was given for decades by Western democracies to the apartheid regime in South Africa. Other examples are the support given by Western democracies to the Shah of Iran and, later, to Saddam Hussein in Iraq.

The idea that most non-democratic nations in the world are safely on the road towards democracy may well be false. In some cases democracy might not evolve at all. In some other cases, it may be stopped from evolving by powerful democratic states protecting their own interests against a democratic development. We should not rely too heavily on recent short-term trends. Even where there is progress, the situation might be suddenly reversed. Finally, even established democracies may be overthrown.

The establishment of a global democracy, along lines to be defended in this book, may provide a strong incentive to the establishment of democracy within all nation-states as well but, in the absence of such an incentive, we cannot take democracy for granted. So even if democracies do now wage war against one another, they may well come to wage (aggressive) war against non-democratic states. It is even more obvious that non-democratic states may continue to wage war against one another as well as against democratic states.

The discussion thus far has focused on wars *between* nation-states. But there are also *civil* wars. We have seen that, since the early nineteenth century, civil wars have been even more numerous than wars between states (with a ratio of 1.3 to 1). They should also be taken into account when we discuss whether, if we want to ascertain that there is peace in the world, a world government would be necessary. Is democracy, once again, a means of ensuring that there would be no civil war?

Again we must enquire into the most plausible explanation behind the existence of civil wars. This is what the *Human Security Report* has to say about them in recent times:

Between 1946 and 1991 there was a twelvefold rise in the number of civil wars – the greatest jump in 200 years. The data suggest that anti-colonialism and the geopolitics of the Cold War were the major determinants of this increase.[17]

If the main reasons behind recent civil wars have been colonialism and the Cold War, then it may seem as if the problem has already been settled. However, this conclusion may be much too simplistic. What we should learn from history, it seems to me, is that the conditions creating civil war may easily re-emerge, in the way they recently did. So we need to consider whether new conditions creating new civil wars may be in the offing. And there are good reasons to be concerned. One aspect of globalisation, stressed by many contemporary thinkers, seems to be that the system of sovereign nation-states that was established in the seventeenth century tends to erode. This is how the 'realist' H. Bull famously puts the point:

In Western Christendom in the Middle Ages ... no ruler or state was sovereign in the sense of being supreme over a given territory and a given segment of the Christian population; each had to share authority with vassals beneath, and with the Pope and (in Germany and Italy) the Holy Roman Emperor above ... If modern states were to come to share their authority over their citizens, and their ability to command their loyalties, on the one hand with regional and world authorities, and on the other hand with sub-state or sub-national authorities, to such an extent that the concept of sovereignty ceased to be applicable, then a neo-mediaeval form of universal political order might be said to have emerged.[18]

If this picture is correct, it may well mean that few wars between democratic states may come to be fought, although now *civil* war may come to be the *main* problem. For there is much evidence to the effect that weak states, even (weak) democracies, tend to engender civil war in a way in which neither strong totalitarian states nor well-established democracies do.[19]

The erosion of the nation-state may come to mean that we encounter many weak democracies. Even formerly peaceful countries, such as Yugoslavia, have proved to be potentially very violent parts of the world. Here the spontaneous *introduction* of democracy after the death of Tito has meant violent war. In Iraq, where a kind of democracy cum occupation (a contradiction in terms?) has been *forcefully* introduced, even more violent conflict, with hundreds of thousands of victims, has ensued. Something similar, if less spectacular, may come to happen in countries in the world where national democracies have been well established, but where they are now, due to globalisation, losing their grip on many important political problems. If there is no higher authority to turn to, conflicts within these states, between different ethnic groups, for example, may well evolve into civil war.

It is true that, recently, we have seen a decrease, not an increase, in the prevalence of civil war. It is noteworthy, however, that this seems in some instances, at least, to be explained by effective repression rendered possible by the existing pax Americana. Once that repression is removed, there is an obvious risk that civil war will ensue once again. If we again come to face a situation in world politics where several superpowers compete for world domination, it is highly likely that wars, such as those from our recent past, will be fought by their respective client states or client factions of existing states on the global arena.

This should not be interpreted as an absolute claim that global peace will *never* come about, if we rely on the internally civilising mechanisms in sovereign nation-states; however, it seems wise to conclude that, if we could establish a world government, this would very much facilitate the establishment of world peace. Yet each year that we postpone the project, many innocent people will get killed. So the argument arising from peace to world government, if not conclusive, has a lot of force indeed.

6. A league of nations – peacemaking and peacekeeping operations

The *Human Security Report* stresses as an important and explaining factor as to why there has been a trend towards more peaceful relations in the world, that the United Nations and other international authorities have been busy creating conditions for peace. This, of course, is perfectly in the spirit of both Bentham (with his diet) and Kant (insisting on the need for a league of nations). This is how the recent efforts are described:

- A sixfold increase in the number of preventive diplomacy missions (those that seek to stop wars from starting) mounted by the UN between 1990 and 2002.
- A fourfold increase in peacemaking activities (those that seek to stop ongoing conflicts) over the same period.
- A sevenfold increase in the number of 'Friends of the Secretary-General', 'Contact Groups' and other government-initiated mechanisms to support peacemaking and peacebuilding missions between 1990 and 2003.
- An elevenfold increase in the number of economic sanctions in place against regimes around the world between 1989 and 2001.
- A fourfold increase in the number of UN peacekeeping operations between 1987 and 1999. The increase in numbers was not the only change. The new missions were, on average, far larger and more complex than those of the Cold War era and they

have been relatively successful in sustaining the peace. With 40% of post-conflict countries relapsing into war again within five years, the importance of preventing wars from restarting is obvious.[20]

Does this show that a world government is not necessary if we want to establish perpetual peace? I think not.

First, even if these measures here depicted have been fairly helpful, this does not show that they would have been sufficient had the situation been only slightly worse. We are here considering a very short phase of our recent history. There is little reason to believe that it is anything but a statistical aberration. Secondly, in spite of the fact that we are experiencing a very special historical period, with a vulnerable pax Americana, there have still been many wars, if not as many as before. We have good reason to assume that, if peacemaking and peacekeeping efforts from the UN have been to some extent efficacious, the measures taken by a world government would have been even more so. Finally, there is no guarantee that, when new conflicts emerge in the world, when the United States world hegemony is seriously threatened by, say, China, international organisations may not come to prove to be completely powerless.

7. Poverty and war

It is only too obvious that one of the factors behind many wars is poverty. We can see this in Africa, where the *Human Security Report* states:

> Almost every country across the broad middle belt of the conti-
> nent – from Somalia in the east to Sierra Leone in the west, from
> Sudan in the north to Angola in the south – remains trapped in a
> volatile mix of poverty, crime, unstable and inequitable political
> institutions, ethnic discrimination, low state capacity and the
> 'bad neighbourhoods' of other crisis-ridden states – all factors
> associated with increased risk of armed conflict.
> The combination of pervasive poverty, declining GDP per

capita, poor infrastructure, weak administration, external inter-
vention and an abundance of cheap weapons, plus the effects of
a major decline in per capita foreign assistance for much of the
1990s, mean that armed conflicts in these countries are difficult
to avoid, contain or end.

Moreover, violent conflict exacerbates the very conditions that
gave rise to it in the first place, creating a classic 'conflict trap'
from which escape is extraordinarily difficult. Unsurprisingly,
sustaining peace settlements is a major challenge in many of
the continent's post-conflict countries.[21]

Even if there are some improvements that can be registered in this
part of the world,[22] it is obvious that we are not here approaching
perpetual peace. This indicates that a way of making the world more
peaceful would be to abolish global injustices and poverty. But can
this be achieved without our having recourse to a world government?
In the next chapter I will argue that it cannot. Furthermore, growing
ecological problems tend both to exacerbate existing conflicts in the
world, and they may well come to engender new problems with
poverty when the price of scarce resources drastically increases, so
it seems that the arguments for a world government from peace,
justice and the environment are closely intertwined.

8. Can we have war with a world government?

If a world government is established, then this world government
will have the monopoly on the use of violence. This means that peace
is secured as long as the government persists. And it is likely that it
will indeed persist, for there is no one who can effectively challenge
it. Of course, there is still some room for terrorism, and even civil war,
but such problems can be handled in most nation-states by respective governments; in a similar vain, they will be handled, on a global
level, by the world government. Also one common reason for civil
war within nation-states will be absent once a world government
has been established. In a world ruled by one sovereign government,
people will not feel that they belong to a suppressed minority in a

nation-state. I return to this when, in Chapter 7, I discuss whether global democracy is desirable as such.

The fact that there is no one who could challenge the global monopoly on the use of violence on the part of the world government may be a reason not to want such a government, but there is no denying that we have good reason to believe that the world government will be able to secure peace.

9. *Conclusion*

It is reasonable to assume that a world government can guarantee perpetual peace. It is also reasonable to assume, as we will see in the following chapter, that its introduction will mean that democracy will spread across the world. It is not, however, reasonable to assume that democracy will spread spontaneously without the establishment of a (democratic) world government, or, at least it is reasonable to believe that, without the establishment of global democracy, the process towards local democracy will be slowed down. But then we cannot rely on the idea that democracies do not wage war against one another as a means to establishing peace around the world.

In some cases democracies may well wage war against one another, and there is no guarantee that they will not wage aggressive war against non-democratic states. Democracies may well come to block the road to democracy in some parts of the world, and even overthrow democracies when it suits their own interests. We know all this from history. It has happened over and over again, and we can deduce from the fact that it has previously happened that it *can* do so again. In addition to this, non-democratic states may come to wage aggressive war against one another and against democracies. Finally, even if, at the end of the day, all nation-states developed democratic systems, and even if this resulted in the end of war around the world, we cannot afford to wait passively for this to happen.

3

The argument arising from global justice

1. Distributive justice

The argument arising from global justice in defence of the establishment of a world government, comes in many different versions depending on which notion of distributive justice is taken as its point of departure. Common to the different notions is the claim that there exist serious global injustices, that is, that the distribution of resources among people around the world is unjust. Facts often referred to, when such a claim can be substantiated, are sometimes given by simple (though, as we will see, somewhat controversial) economic statistics, such as those given by the World Bank and the United Nations, to the effect that of a global population of more than 6 billion, about one-fifth, or 1.2 billion, live on less than one US dollar per day, and nearly half, or 2.8 billion, live on less than two US dollars per day. There are also, however, simple (and not at all controversial) facts concerning health that are often pointed to, with respect to life expectancy, under-five mortality and maternal mortality. For example, life expectancy in Sierra Leone is thirty-five years, in Angola and Malawi thirty-six years, in Zambia and Zimbabwe it is thirty-seven years. Although these are the only countries in which life expectancy is less than forty years, there are thirty countries in which life expectancy is less than fifty years. This can be compared with countries like Australia, Japan, Sweden and

Switzerland where life expectancy is more than eighty years. The pattern is no different with respect to the under-five mortality rate. In Denmark, Iceland, Norway, Singapore and Sweden, fewer than five out of 1,000 children will die before they reach the age of five. In Sierra Leone the rate is 316 and fifty countries have a rate greater than 100. Finally, while the number of women who die of causes related to their pregnancies is five out of 100,000 in Kuwait, Sweden and Switzerland, women face grave risks in some other countries. In the Central African Republic, Malawi, Mozambique, Rwanda and Sierra Leone the maternal mortality rate is greater than 1,000 in 100,000. The 1 per cent risk of death is repeated with each pregnancy.[1]

What does it mean to state that this global situation is unjust? Are there both moral problems and problems to do with justice? I think not. To say that the distribution is unjust is merely a way of saying that redistribution ought to take place. Problems of justice are *moral* problems, to wit, moral problems to do with *distribution*.

Which are the injustices, then? The answer people tend to give to this question depends on the moral theory from which they start. There is no need in the present context to try to sort out which moral theory is the correct one. I have my own opinion about this, but I will not try to defend it in the present context. There is no need to do so, since *all*, or nearly all, plausible moral theories tend to identify a common feature of today's world as unjust. No very subtle argument is needed to substantiate this claim. Here I will focus in my discussion on three different approaches to distributive justice: utilitarianism; egalitarianism; and moral rights theory.

2. Utilitarianism

Let us first take utilitarianism (my own favoured position). It might be thought that a utilitarian has problems in handling justice, since the utilitarian does not hold that any pattern of distribution is desirable as such. The utilitarian focuses instead on the sum total of well-being on the globe.[2] According to utilitarianism, if an action does not maximise the sum total of well-being, it is wrong. However, even if the utilitarian is not interested in equality, or particularly in the lot of those who are worst off, *as such*, the utilitarian does want a distribution resulting in the largest possible sum total of well-being. We know from economists that, to a very large extent, there is a diminishing marginal utility in material things. In particular, as we have seen, poverty seems to correlate almost perfectly with poor health, a short life expectancy, under-five mortality and maternal mortality. So the fact that 1 billion people in the world live in terrible conditions, and the fact that 2.8 billion people live in abject poverty (on less than two US dollars a day) is a good reason to suspect that the world's material resources could be spent in a more efficient way (as we shall see these exact figures have been questioned, but this does not make any *significant* difference).

The utilitarian does not object to inequality as such, the utilitarian does not dislike the fact that some people have very good living conditions as such, but the utilitarian must protest when scarce resources are wasted on rich people who cannot transform them into 'happiness' in the way that poor people would be able to do. Therefore, there is no denying that, from a utilitarian point of view, the poverty of more than two billion people worldwide is an injustice, given one big proviso: that there is something we can do about the problem. If not, then, from a moral point of view, poverty is no problem. This has to do with the fact that utilitarians agree with Kant when he insists that 'ought' implies 'can'. This means that if we *cannot* solve a problem, we are under no moral obligation to do so.

3. Egalitarianism

If utilitarianism has a problem with the distribution of resources around the globe in general and, in particular, with the fact that more than two billion people live in abject poverty, then all sorts of egalitarian theories have even more serious problems with the fact. Such views come in two main versions: one focuses on the distributional pattern, that is, on differences between those who are well off and those who are not, and even sometimes on the variation in between these groups (relational views); and the other focuses exclusively on those who are, absolutely speaking, worst off (the priority view).

In their most plausible versions, the relational view and the priority view share the assumption that what, in the final analysis, should be distributed in a certain way is well-being, not material resources. This may be of little interest to those who hold the priority view, since those who are worst off are so both in terms of material resources and well-being. Also, according to the priority view, it is indeed bad news to learn that, between 1965 and 1998, even though the income in the poorest nations containing one-fifth of the world's population more than doubled, *in 16 of the world's poorest countries average per capita income has fallen.*[3]

The law of diminishing marginal utility of material resources may mean, however, that the *differences* in well-being are not as extensive as it may seem when we consider the material aspect of a distribution. Those who command most resources may be very poor at transforming these resources into 'happiness'. This may mean that, from the relational point of view, the world is not as unjust as it may seem when we focus on material resources. However, there is no denying that rich people are better off than those who live in abject poverty, so, even on the relational view, the world is unjust.

If a version of the priority view is on the right track, then there is reason to improve the lot of those more than two billion people who live in abject poverty. In particular we ought to focus on those among them who are, absolutely speaking, worst off. It may seem that, in the relational view, we have two options. We could either improve the lot of those who are worst off or worsen the situation for those who are best off. But, if we want to stick to a version of egalitarianism that is plausible, then only the first option is open to us. So on all plausible versions of egalitarianism, we must conclude that the world is grossly unjust. The existence of 2.8 billion people living in abject poverty (where the rest live in more decent conditions, and where at least one billion live in affluence) is what makes it unjust.

Perhaps the utilitarians and egalitarians could be more complacent if there was evidence to show that the differences are going away. Are there any signs that they are doing so? This is an extremely complicated question to answer, since the answer depends heavily on how you assess the material situation of people, on what measurements of inequality you employ and on whether you are interested merely in relative differences or if you are also interested in absolute differences. The Swedish economist Peter Svedberg has produced, to my knowledge, the best survey of all these studies. Before going into his review of his results, let us consider some methodological points he is raising (here recapitulated in a very simplified form).

First, if we measure the economic situation of people around the world in terms of how many American dollars the citizens of a country have per capita (a standard procedure in the literature), it makes a considerable difference if you adjust for differences in purchasing power parity (PPP) across countries, or if you just rely on the current exchange rates. It seems to be received wisdom today among development economists that it is better to rely on PPP-adjusted dollars (P$), which, it should be noted, has not been done in the study for the World Bank and the United Nations referred to above. However, it is also received wisdom that when you adopt this procedure, you then run the risk of mitigating real differences. Let us here make a conservative estimate, however, and rely only on investigations measuring economic situation in this manner (relying on PPP-adjusted dollars).

There are then the different measurements of inequality, some of them focusing only on the difference between the most affluent and those who are worst off, others paying attention also to the total variation on the globe. It is a moral question which kind of measurement makes most sense. There is no need to go into this discussion here, however, since, on neither account is it possible to paint a very optimistic scenario.

Finally, even if relative differences may seem to be most important, let us also consider what is happening in the world to absolute differences. Even those who do not find such differences of immediate moral importance must admit that, if they are glaring, they may have very bad side-effects.

Now, what is happening to the situation in the world? This is how Svedberg summarises it:

The argument arising from global justice

The first conclusion is that since the 1960s, the relative inter-national distribution of income, as measured by Gini and other comprehensive indicators, has remained rather stable. Most of the about 10 studies providing estimates for a long period, based on P$ income data, have found a decline in the –0.02 to –0.05 interval. A few studies have estimated global distribution, i.e. also taking intra-country distribution into consideration, and found it to be more uneven than inter-national distribution. Most of these studies also suggest that global relative distribution has remained largely unaltered over the past few decades (a change in the ±0.02–0.03 range).[4]

Moreover, if we focus exclusively on those who are at the top and those who are at the bottom, the long-term picture is even gloomier:

A final conclusion regarding inter-country distribution is that there has been a marked increase in the relative difference in per-capita income between the absolutely poorest countries, almost all in Sub-Saharan Africa, and the richest countries (primarily within the OECD area), since the 1960s. This is shown most clearly by investigations based on income ratio measures, but also by those using comprehensive distribution measures ... As noted in several studies, the lack of growth in most African countries should be the main concern, not only for world income distribution, but considering the sharply increasing poverty.

Finally, if we consider the *absolute* differences between those who are the richest and those who are the poorest, the future is extremely problematic:

There are no signs that economic growth in the rich countries is grinding to a halt, or even slowing down. This means that although the poorest countries may manage to increase their per capita growth rates to the level thus far proven to be the highest possible (about 6 per cent annually for a long period),

35

the absolute income gap will continue to widen for several decades. If today's poor countries 'only' manage to grow a couple of percentage points quicker than the rich nations, there will be no decline in the absolute income gaps until some time in the 22nd century.

It is tempting to argue that absolute differences do not matter once those who are poorest are above a certain level. However, as is pointed out by Svedberg, if those who are most affluent in a poor country identify with those who are most affluent in a rich country, they may tend to migrate to the rich country, in spite of the fact that they can live a good life in the poor country. 'Brain drain' will be engendered by the absolute difference.

Could not the egalitarians and prioritarians trust an often mentioned mechanism: economic growth. Can we not rely on the idea that economic growth is bound, in the long term, to create equal conditions? No, according to Svedberg:

> One of the contending issues is whether there is a general tendency for income distribution within countries to become more unequal over time in the wake of economic growth and globalisation. Extended and improved data now allow this question to be addressed for some 50 countries. The estimates suggest that in a few countries, income distribution has turned significantly more uneven, and in another small number of countries, significantly more even. In the great majority of the 50 countries, however, income distribution, measured in different ways, has remained more or less unaltered between the individual years compared.

It seems then, that the world is deeply and robustly unjust. All egalitarians, of the relative as well as of the prioritarian variety, must conclude that something should be done to rectify the injustices. They must be addressed in a direct manner.

Once again, however, we must draw this conclusion with one big proviso: unless there is something we can do to change the situation, we are not allowed to speak of it as unjust. Brute natural differences may be something to lament, but they do not create a moral problem until the moment has come when there is something we can do to eliminate them. This is true no less of egalitarianism, in both its versions, than it is of utilitarianism.

4. *The moral rights view*

The third influential view of justice and morality is very different. I refer here to the moral rights tradition, according to which morality (justice) is a matter of respecting (negative) rights. According to this tradition we own ourselves and we own what we have acquired in an appropriate manner. These rights are negative. They make up a kind of fence around each individual, a fence that should not be trespassed by anyone else. No one should be killed, unless he has commissioned someone to kill him, no one should be robbed of his property. Nevertheless, there is no positive right for a person in distress to be assisted. Of course, if something that belongs to me has been taken from me, I have a right to redress. However, if I just happen to be poor, then I have no right to a moral complaint against those who happen to be better off.

It might be thought that in this view of justice there is little to complain about in today's world. Could it not be argued that most of the more than two billion people who live in abject poverty suffer from bad luck rather than injustice? If this is true, then, according to the moral rights theory (as here described), their plight does not constitute any moral problem. However, there are two observations that are crucial to the assessment of the claim that those who live in abject poverty are simply unlucky. One has to do with the fact that those who have been robbed of their belongings have a right to redress. If it can be shown that much of the poverty in the world is due to earlier rights violations, then those who are worst off may well have a morally legitimate claim on those who are better off (because they hold property that they have inherited from those who stole it).

The other observation has to do with what has become known as

Locke's proviso. John Locke designed a moral rights theory which bears similarities to that outlined roughly here, but Locke made the important proviso that, when originally an individual acquires property that is not owned by anyone (or, perhaps, by God, or by all in common), then he must leave 'enough and as good … in common for others'.[5] Adherents of more radical and up-to-date versions of the moral rights theory have accepted this also, in particular Robert Nozick in his *Anarchy, State, and Utopia* where, however, he takes a rather liberal interpretation of Locke's proviso. According to Nozick, the crucial thing is that others do *not have their situation worsened* by the acquisition.[6] This means that, even if there is no oil left for anyone when all the resources have been privatised this does not mean that the proviso is not fulfilled. If those who cannot own oil have their living conditions improved because of the existence of the oil industry, then they do not have any justified complaint to make against the owners of the oil industry.

For the sake of the argument, let us accept this liberal reading of the proviso. Where, from the point of view of justice, does all this leave the more than two billion people living in abject poverty? I think it clear that their existence (their plight) does constitute a problem for the moral rights theory. For, to a large extent, it is certainly true that many aspects of their poverty have their roots in past violations of the rights of their ancestors. This is most conspicuously the case with many aboriginal peoples, who have simply been robbed of all or most of the land and sea and other resources they once controlled (or 'owned', even if they did not necessarily employ any notion of private ownership). It is also equally obvious that when various acquisitions of property have been made in the past, enough and as good has not been left for people in poor and exploited countries to acquire. When natural resources have, literally speaking, been taken away from poor countries, those no longer exist to be exploited by those who now inhabit these countries, and, judging from their material situation, it is obvious that there has not been adequate compensation for this loss.

I have a vivid personal experience of this. A few years ago I travelled in Bolivia, one of the poorest countries in South America, where I visited two mines. First, I visited a modern gold mine at Uroro, where a North American firm had exploited a gold finding. They were just finalising their job and about to leave. As a matter of fact, with modern machinery, they had taken away an entire mountain of gold. It was obvious that there was little gain made for people in the vicinity, let alone in Bolivia at large. No compensation had been paid for the loss. There was just waste land left. I then went to silver mine in Cerro Rico at Potosi. The mine had been abandoned by big business and it had now been taken over by a workers' cooperative. I went deep into a narrow pit, a terrible experience for a spoiled person such as myself. The workers used sledgehammers and spits. They transported their fellow workers from one pit to another with the aid of a bucket tied to a wire. Certainly, I learnt from them that, enough and as good had not been left for them. The poor mine could hardly sustain their living.

These two examples are typical of many of the poor nations in the world. So I believe that we must conclude that, even when judged from the point of view of the moral rights theory, the existence of more than two billion people living in abject poverty does constitute an injustice – provided once again that there is something one can do to improve their lot. This is true no less from the point of view of the moral rights theory than from utilitarianism and egalitarianism.

Is there anything one can do in order to improve the lot of those who are worst off? Could a world government improve their lot? Could it be improved without a world government? Let me reverse the order of the argument here and start with moral rights theories, and then proceed to prioritarianism and utilitarianism.

5. Is global justice a feasible goal? The moral rights answer

According to the moral rights theory of justice, the existing injustices are the result of rights violations in the past. Original owners have been robbed of their legitimate holdings, and original acquisitions have been made that are at variance with Locke's proviso, even in its liberal interpretation. What is needed, therefore, is restitution of a kind. It seems clear that, in principle, a world government should be capable of managing the problem. But is there no way of handling it without resorting to a world government?

Could a free global market do the trick? What if all nation-states agree to a system of perfectly free global trade, would such a system result in prosperity for all? The idea that it would seems to me to be naive. Typically, wealthy nations have gained economic strength and built their wealth through astute forms of protectionism. Some protectionism is probably needed in order for the poor nations in today's world to catch up with those who are ahead of them in economic, social and political development. They would profit if wealthy nations refrained from protection *against* them, of course, but this is probably not sufficient in order to make them prosper. Irrespective of whether this is so or not, from a moral rights perspective it is not sufficient that differences are levelled out over the long term, those who have had their rights violated should be *compensated*, and this is not something we could expect a free market to accomplish.

Moreover, even if a free global market could do the trick, in the very distant future, the problem is that we who now live will all be dead. Nevertheless, moral rights theory is highly demanding. It is not sufficient that justice is achieved in the long run. Those who have been wronged have a right to an immediate, or at least very speedy, restitution. This seems indeed impossible unless a world government is established.

The point here is not logical but practical. *In principle* one could have all sorts of elaborate forms of international law and legal adjudication without the existence of a global state. In the spirit of the legal philosopher, H. L. A. Hart,[7] one could argue that legal validity does not require sovereignty. But when important economic interests are at stake, such international law will have no real teeth unless backed up by a sovereign world government. The problem is that when national governments try to escape from international economic demands, irrespective of the matter of legal validity, they tend to gain support, rather than criticism, from 'their own' populations.

Somewhat unexpectedly, then, the moral rights perspective is a perspective that very clearly indicates that, if we could improve the lot of the poorest through a world government, we should opt for a world government. It must be added, however, that if we want to stick to a moral rights perspective, we had better see to it that the global state, once established, is a *minimal* state, restricting its mandate to upholding global respect for human rights and, when violations do take place, to rectify injustices and compensate victims.

6. Is global justice a feasible goal? The prioritarian answer

John Rawls is famous for having argued that:

> All social primary goods – liberty and opportunity, income and wealth, and the bases of self-respect – are to be distributed equally unless an unequal distribution of any or all of these goods is to be to the advantage of the least favoured.[8]

This is a version of Rawls' 'difference principle', and it seems to place him among those who adhere to the priority view. It appears to make him a very radical adherent of the priority view, since he insists on a 'lexical' reading of his principle. If there is *any* way of improving the lot of those who are worst off, this should be done, *whatever the costs to those who are better off*.

It is tempting to apply this principle to the world at large and to argue, then, that gross injustices exist in the world. Rawls himself has hesitated to do so, however. In *A Theory of Justice* he did not discuss problems of global justice, he took it for granted that his principle should be applied to nation-states. However, in *The Law of Peoples*, he developed a theory of global justice in two stages: first, there is a contract among individuals to form a nation; and secondly, representatives of the various nations agree to a second contract, where the difference principle is rejected on the global level.

What Rawls proposes is merely the following:

1. Peoples are free and independent, and their freedom and independence are to be respected by other peoples.

2. Peoples are to observe treaties and undertakings.
3. Peoples are equal and are parties to the agreements that bind them.
4. Peoples are to observe a duty of non-intervention.
5. Peoples have the right of self-defense but no right to instigate war for reasons other than self-defense.
6. Peoples are to honor human rights.
7. Peoples are to observe certain specified restrictions in the conduct of war.
8. Peoples have a duty to assist other peoples living under unfavorable conditions that prevent their having a just or decent political and social regime.[9]

The crucial point here is (8). Why does Rawls restrict himself to a 'duty to assist' other peoples? Why does he not want to apply the difference principle on a global level? At least part of Rawls' reasoning seems to be founded on scepticism with respect to necessary administrative resources and a fear of a world government, which would be necessary if we want to solve these administrative problems. He believes that, unless a world government is established, the difference principle cannot be implemented and he doesn't want a world government to be established.

Rawls does not go deeply into a discussion about world government. With reference to Kant, he merely dismisses the idea of a world government with the comment that it will lead either to 'global despotism' or 'rule over a fragile empire torn by frequent civil strife'.[10] I will discuss the problem of whether a world government, in a democratic form (global democracy) is desirable in its own right in a later chapter. My belief is that it is desirable in its own right, not merely as a means to global justice.

The former concern, that there will be insufficient administrative resources, unless a world government is established, seems to me to be plausible. I will discuss it when I ponder whether Thomas Pogge has found a way of meeting this kind of scepticism. It should be noted, however, that if we conceive of the difference principle as stating an ideal of justice, we might still rely on it when we assess the global situation with respect to justice. It then surfaces that the situation in the world is terribly unjust, and this means that those who want to follow Rawls and reject the idea of a world government, must acknowledge that there is an enormous price in terms of justice for their rejection. At least this is so if there is really no way of accomplishing global justice without resorting to a world government.

Some thinkers have suggested that there are ways of achieving global justice without resorting to a world government. Thomas Pogge has made the most ambitious, and also the most influential, attempt.[11] He has discussed many ways in which the situation of those living in abject poverty in the world can be improved, most recently with respect to how medicines should be provided to them, but his most radical suggestion to this effect was made some years ago. I refer here to his suggestion that there is a way of attacking global injustices through the introduction of a tax upon the use of natural resources (a global resources tax, 'GRT'), and global distribution of the proceeds raised by it, solving the problem with 'inadequate administrative capabilities and the dangers of a world government'.[12]

I am not quite certain to what Pogge's personal view of world government really amounts. It is possible that he may very well be sympathetic to the idea.[13] However, in his discussion of a GRT he accepts, at least for the sake of his argument, John Rawls' Kantian scepticism with respect to a world government. So in his discussion, it is assumed that a system of nation-states is in place and that national governments are in control of the resources of their respective nation. When these resources are exploited, the tax must be paid, if not, sanctions will be initiated. However, these sanctions do not come from a world government. Instead, they could be decentralised:

> They could work as follows: Once the agency facilitating the flow of GRT payments reports that a country has not met its obligations under the scheme, all other countries are required to impose duties on imports from, and perhaps also similar levies

on exports to, this country to raise funds equivalent to its GRT obligations plus the cost of these enforcement measures.[14]

Would a tax system along these lines work in the absence of a world government? Would it meet the demands from global justice?

I cannot see any reason why it could not work in the absence of a world government if representatives of most countries agreed to establish it. It is, however, extremely difficult to believe that representatives of the most affluent countries would agree to establish it. Moreover, would it make much of a difference from the point of view of global justice? Pogge is very optimistic on this count:

> In light of today's vast global social and economic inequalities, one may think that a massive GRT scheme would be necessary to support global background justice. But I do not think this is so. Current inequalities are the cumulative result of decades and centuries in which the more-developed peoples used their advantages in capital and knowledge to expand these advantages ever further. They show the power of long-term compounding rather than overwhelmingly powerful centrifugal tendencies of our global market system. Even a rather small GRT may then be sufficient continuously to balance these ordinary centrifugal tendencies of market systems enough to prevent the development of excessive inequalities and to maintain in equilibrium a rough global distributional profile that preserves global background justice.[15]

This may be true. But what it shows is not that a GRT can be a method of establishing global justice, only that it can be a means of preserving a global background justice. And this is of little avail in a world where such a background justice is what is missing. My point here is not that there are faults in Pogge's argument. For the sake of his argument, he labours under strict assumptions given by Rawls; in particular, he assumes that the origin behind the division of the world into nation-states involves no injustice. If we relax these restrictions and turn to the real world we realise, I submit that the

GRT as such is not a method of *establishing* justice in a deeply unjust world.

Pogge stresses that the system should be designed to serve the interests of the poor. The rules should be such that 'the entire GRT scheme has the maximum possible positive impact on the world's poorest persons – the poorest quintile, say – in the long run'. In particular, they 'must make it clear to members of the political and economic elite of GRT-eligible countries that, if they want their society to receive GRT funds, they must cooperate in making those funds effective toward enhancing the opportunities and the standard of living of the domestic poor'.[16]

This sounds fine, as far as it goes, but rules are one thing, how they operate in real life can be something very different. What if a corrupt government in a third world country uses the GRT funds for their own private purposes? Pogge answers this concern by suggesting even more rules. He suggests that, 'a country might receive 60 percent of the GRT funds it is eligible for, one third of this through the government and two-thirds of it through other channels'. These rules are 'to be designed ... by an international group of economists and international lawyers'.[17]

This looks very much like a move in the direction of world government. The national sovereignty of third world countries is flouted. So perhaps we need a world government, not only to get the system of GRT in place, but also to see to it that it operates in the manner it was designed to do. And once again, one may wonder whether such a system is sufficient if we want to establish a global background situation of justice, rather than maintaining one that is already in place.

I think not. This is not only, or mainly, a problem with scales. The problem is rather that the schema focuses too much on redistribution of resources (in too modest a scale, moreover) and too little on power relations. Even if we could assemble international groups of distinguished and impartial economists and lawyers, these groups would not be able to prevent resources being wasted when redistributed in this way. Local corrupt governments and representatives of transnational firms, backed, or at least tolerated, by governments in rich countries will conspire together against the system. Moreover, the money gathered in this manner will be a drop in the ocean when it comes to the establishment, rather than just the preservation, of a situation of global background justice. Tax policies and other measures in the rich countries will annihilate the positive effects of the system.

What is needed then to achieve global justice? I return to this question in the final section of this chapter. Let me for now just conclude that the most ambitious attempt thus far to show that global justice can be achieved, without any resort to a world government, seems to fail.

7. Is global justice a feasible goal? The utilitarian answer

Utilitarianism is the view that the end (maximisation of the sum total of well-being) justifies the means, so a utilitarian will have no principled problems with accepting a world government as the means to addressing the problem of global justice. We have seen that such injustices do exist, and we have found reasons to believe that they will not go away, not even if a global policy of free trade could be established. Another more robust approach must be taken to them. We could resort to a world government. But before we do, let us consider one more possibility. Would not the problem with global injustice be solved if all nation-states were not only democratised but also transformed into socialism? A utilitarian would, no more than an egalitarian, have any *principled* objections to socialism. In this these views differ from radical forms of moral rights theory.

This idea that socialism should do the trick may seem very far-fetched in a situation where many socialist systems have recently been abolished and replaced with capitalist ones. I also agree that it would be to wait in vain for the world to turn socialist in the manner we know from, say, the former Soviet Union. But are there no better socialist alternatives available? As a matter of fact I think there are. I think here of various forms of market socialist systems. The most elaborate and interesting one among them, as far as I know, is the one that has been put forward and defended by the American philosopher and mathematician, David Schweickart, most effectively in his recent book *After Capitalism*. For the sake of brevity I will focus exclusively on this example.

This is a version of socialism, or economic democracy, retaining from the Soviet experiment the idea that the means of production should be socialised (that is, owned by the state), but adding that workers' cooperatives should be allowed to use them (wage labour would thus be abolished – something which goes beyond the Soviet experiment) and produce for a market (which is different, of course, from the Soviet experiment and equal to capitalism). Publicly-owned banks would provide the means of investment to workers' cooperatives, gathering the necessary means through taxation on the resources used by the workers' self-managed firms.

This is not the place to go into details, but it is amazing how strong a case can be made for this kind of economic system. It is attractive from a democratic point of view, and there are good reasons to believe that it will be at least as innovative as capitalism but less prone to expand the output of production (more inclined to allow for leisure rather than consumption), and as efficient as capitalism when it comes to the allocation of resources. Moreover, it has a tendency to produce more egalitarian conditions within the country where it is established. According to Schweickart, it should be established on a national level. He shows no sympathy with cosmopolitan ideas. The nation-states would be retained, even after they have each and every one of them gone through a socialist revolution. And he is very optimistic indeed about the capacity of a system of socialist nation-states to eliminate economic injustices, both within nation-states and in the world at large.

To some (to a large, as a matter of fact) extent I am prepared to accept Schweickart's optimistic assessments, given that socialism can be established in the manner he indicates in all nation-states. We should keep in mind that the economic system around the world that has been most effective in the most recent decades with respect to the increased creation of wealth is the Chinese state-market system (very different from the one delineated by Schweickart, to be sure, but also very different from a traditional capitalist one). So

47

it is not very far-fetched to believe that there may exist all sorts of different models, this being one among them, that are superior to 'pure', or 'real', capitalism. However, even if Schweickart's assessments are basically right and, even if, at the end of the day, it will prove possible in the manner indicated by him to eliminate global injustices in a piecemeal way, by eliminating them in each nation-state, I think that, realistically, we must acknowledge that the day when socialism is thus established in all nation-states in the world is rather distant. Even if the socialist system is superior to capitalism, which I do believe it is, and even if it would be stable, once put in place, which I also believe it would, there are so many very strong and powerful interests that are likely to go to all necessary lengths to block the road to socialism.

The existing capitalist order represents a kind of equilibrium. Even if there exists a possible, superior equilibrium, that is, the socialist one, the coordination problems when we move in that direction are formidable. So for the foreseeable future we must take it for granted that those who do not want to walk down this road, and who possess enormous power assets, will succeed in blocking it.

Furthermore, even if socialism were established in each nation-state, there would remain global injustices to tackle; perhaps they could be negotiated away between free states, but there is no denying that, possibly, a world government could be an additional means when it comes to dealing with them. Once a basic global system of justice was established, something like Pogge's global resource tax might be a sufficient means to retain the existing order, but, even in a world of socialist countries, it is likely that it would be insufficient when it comes to *establishing* global justice.

So, from the point of view of global economic justice, also when we assess the situation through the application of utilitarianism, we have good reasons to see whether there are any more immediate means of fighting the injustices in the absence of socialism in most nation-states in the world. We need to look to the world government and investigate in what way it can handle the problem.

8. World government and the road to global justice

Utilitarians and prioritarians have both placed much stress on the obligation of rich people to give away some share of their wealth to those who are poorest, and various different institutional structures have been designed which are intended to render possible the transactions of resources that are necessary. Pogge's global resource tax is just one example of this. Peter Singer[18] and Peter Unger[19] are other examples that come to mind. These authors argue convincingly that we have a duty to assist people in distress, even if they live a long distance from ourselves. I share their opinion. That is why the royalties from this book will go entirely to Oxfam. However, it is not likely that people at large will do their moral duty. And note that their point is that, given that *most* people do *not* give away all their wealth, *each* has a heavy obligation to do so. It is not clear what would happen if most people actually gave away all their wealth – perhaps economic disaster would result.

So there is something deeply problematic with this focus on redistribution through taxes and foreign aid. In order to solve the problems that are indeed gigantic, such a tax or system of aid would also have to be gigantic — and yet tempered in order not to destroy the world economy. But is it reasonable to assume that heavy global taxes, even if they were suitable for their task, will ever be accepted? According the moral rights approach, such heavy global taxes are themselves suspect unless they can be conceived of as rectifications of past injustices. But setting this problem to one side, is there any possibility that people will be prepared to pay them? I think not. I feel little sympathy with communitarian political philosophical thinking in general, but I do think that those communitarians who insist in particular that a welfare state requires a kind of deep solidarity, which cannot easily flourish on a global level, are perfectly right.[20] We may be able to raise the necessary funds in order to deal with the problems created by global warming, where the liability of the populations in the rich part of the world is so obvious, but it is unlikely that we will in the foreseeable future have a global system of redistribution that comes close to the one we have in welfare states such as those in Scandinavia. The problem with such systems is not *only* that they require solidarity among the people living within them; it is also a problem of scales. These systems do redistribute between individuals, but, even more, they distribute resources over the life cycle of each individual. This is part of the reason why they are felt to be acceptable. However, redistribution over the life cycle of each individual on the globe on this scale is not feasible. Therefore, this means that redistribution between individuals on a global scale is also not feasible.

Does all this mean that there is no way in which to abolish global injustices without a world government and that there is no way of abolishing them with a world government? I think this is too pessimistic. However, we must mainly find other ways of combating injustices than having recourse to redistribution of economic resources. The main idea, as was adumbrated above, is to use the world government to create better conditions for *local* struggle for global justice.

The most immediate objective would be to get rid of the subsidies to farming in rich countries, and to abolish all tariffs on the exports from poor countries to rich countries. This does not mean that completely free trade should be established worldwide. That would not be fair. It is reasonable to assume that poor countries will need import tariffs on some products in order to help them establish national industries, making substitution for import possible. Perhaps this can be accomplished without resort to a world government, but, certainly, the existence of a world government would render easier such a reform. It should not be difficult to gain strong support for such a policy among poor people around the world, and they would have little difficulty in showing people in affluent societies that such a solution would be only fair. After all, they could refer to what US President, Ulysses S. Grant once observed:

> For centuries England has relied on protection, has carried it to extremes and has obtained satisfactory results from it. There is no doubt that it is to this system that it owes its present strength. After two centuries, England had found it convenient to adopt

free trade, because it thinks that protection can no longer afford it anything. Very well, Gentlemen, my knowledge of my country leads me to believe that within two hundred years, when America has gotten all it can out of protection, it too will adopt free trade.[21]

Even more important with respect to a world government dealing with global economic justice, would be to see to it that large transnational companies cannot blackmail local governments into accepting poor workplace conditions and wages in exchange for foreign investment. The world government should protect the right of trade unions, provide legislation about minimum wages, prosecute both those who bribe and those who accept bribes when business transactions are made, and so forth.

Is it realistic to assume that a world government will do all this? Would there not be pressure from powerful economic interests urging it to be lenient with respect to big business and to keep the market 'free'? There will certainly be all sorts of pressure groups operating, pressure both pro and con the kinds of measures I have indicated. But since there exists a sound rationale behind them, and since, if they are impartially operated, they give no *differential* incentives to any big business, it is likely that a world government could at least approximate the kind of system which I have adumbrated.

After all, this kind of process has taken place *within* many affluent nation-states, not without some opposition from capitalist groups, but successfully, so why should it be seen as impossible on a *global* level? A prerequisite for this happening is, of course, that there is no way for capitalist interests to threaten that, unless they have their way, they will move elsewhere. Given that a world government has been successfully established there is no place for them to move into any more.[22] Hence the crucial thing is not a direct transfer of economic resources, but a radical change of the global situation with respect to *power*. Once poor people in the world become empowered, both collectively and individually, they will hopefully see to it themselves that their economic situation improves. Indeed, it is incumbent upon the world government to see to it that they do become empowered.

However, even if the use of direct transfers is not the main road to improving the present situation of those who are (relatively or absolutely) poor in the world, there is also room for such transfers. In particular, if we believe that some kind of democratic, perhaps market, socialist system will in the end prove superior to capitalism, a way of advancing on the road to this kind of socialism would be to have a global investment fund subsidising the establishment of worker-controlled firms worldwide, in particular in areas and countries where little private capital is presently being invested. Such firms could, if protected by some import tariffs, come to grow and initiate economic development. Together with other political measures this may mean that there will also be economic development in these areas and countries.

One caveat is in place here. In very special circumstances, of a kind to be discussed in the following chapter, where the lifestyle of a rich minority in the world threatens to cause disaster for people living in poorer parts of the world, I think it both reasonable and, if a world government is in place, feasible, with redistributions of resources in order to make up for what has gone astray in the past. However, this is the exception, not the rule, if my view of the situation is correct.

I admit that what has been said here is not a complete blueprint, but merely a sketch. There may exist other policies that a world government could adopt that would be superior to those I have adumbrated. There are certainly many other measures, besides the ones I have here mentioned, that it could adopt. But how to deal with poverty is one of the three main things that global politics should be about (the other two concern peace and the environment, respectively). Different and often conflicting approaches when it comes to solving the problem of global injustice is only what we should expect, and it is only natural that global political parties of the kind I will adumbrate in a later chapter, will adopt different stances with respect to global justice and compete for the support of the world population for their respective ideas.

4
The environment

1. Global environmental problems

Some problems to do with the environment arise on a global scale. That most discussed one in recent times is, of course, global warming. No nation is solely responsible for it, although some countries are responsible for more of the ill effects than others; collectively we produce greenhouse gases and, hence, the negative effects on the climate. Another problem has to do with scarce natural resources. No single person is individually using up any particular remaining resource, but together we do so (even if, once again, some use much more than do others). The remaining global oil reserves are a much discussed example, while water is perhaps of even greater importance. A third problem has to do with endangered species and the possibility that they will become extinct. Although one person may be responsible for killing the last specimen of such a species, the road leading up to this event is, however, typically walked by us together. These are all well-known and much discussed examples. Others, though not apparent yet, are likely to be forthcoming in the future.

It is obvious, therefore, that global environmental problems need to be solved. However, it is not obvious that we have to resort to a world government in order to do so. Do we? Let us discuss the three aforementioned types of problems in order.

2. *Global warming*

According to the *Third Assessment Report* of the Intergovernmental Panel on Climate Change (IPCC), global warming is a fact. Nine of the ten hottest years during the last 140 years have occurred since 1990 and temperatures are rising at three times the rate of the early 1900s.[1] This is not a mere statistical variation. The report found 'new and stronger evidence that most of the warming observed over the last 50 years is attributable to human activities'.[2] Recently the result has been confirmed by the *Fourth Assessment Report* which stated:

Warming of the climate system is unequivocal, as is now evident from observations of increases in global average air and ocean temperatures, widespread melting of snow and ice, and rising global average sea level.

Eleven of the last twelve years (1995–2006) rank among the 12 warmest years in the instrumental record of global surface temperature (since 1850). The updated 100-year linear trend (1906–2005) of 0.74 [0.56 to 0.92]°C is therefore larger than the corresponding trend for 1901–2000 given in the TAR of 0.6 [0.4 to 0.8]°C.

The linear warming trend over the last 50 years (0.13 [0.10 to 0.16]°C per decade) is nearly twice that for the last 100 years. The total temperature increase from 1850–1899 to 2001–2005 is 0.76 [0.57 to 0.95]°C. Urban heat island effects are real but local, and have a negligible influence.[3]

What will be the consequences of the process? There is no need to go into detail here, we all know from the media what is likely to happen. As oceans become warmer, hurricanes and tropical storms that are now largely confined to the tropics will move further from the equator, hitting large urban areas that have not been built to cope with them. Tropical diseases will become more widespread. Food production will rise in some regions, especially in the high northern latitudes, and fall in others, including sub-Saharan Africa. Sea levels will rise.

As is pointed out by Peter Singer in his book, *One World*, rich nations may be able to cope with these changes, poor nations will not:

> Bangladesh, the world's most densely populated large country, has the world's largest system of deltas and mudflats, where mighty rivers like the Ganges and the Brahmaputra reach the sea. The soil in these areas is fertile, but the hazards of living on such low-lying land are great ... if sea levels continue to rise, many farmers will have no land left. As many as 70 million people could be affected in Bangladesh, and a similar number in China.[4]

Diseases will spread, and it can be envisaged that all sorts of problems will follow in the aftermath to this kind of development.

It is true that all these putative facts have been contested. Even the *Fourth Assessment Report* leaves *some* hope for those who believe that climate change has little to do with our lifestyle. However, it seems to be sound policy to take them seriously. Those who question them are in the minority and the scientific community seems largely to support them. The recent assessment report states that it is 'very likely' – or a more than ninety per cent chance – that human activities, led by burning fossil fuels, are to blame for warming since 1950, while the previous report in 2001 said the link was 'likely', or at least a sixty-six per cent likelihood. This does not mean that, in the final analysis, all the pessimistic prophesies will be borne out by reality, but it does mean that, when designing practical policies, these concerns cannot be put to one side. So how can these putative risks be met?

In principle, if we take the risks for real, there seem to be two achievable ways of meeting those risks. One would be to follow the lead of the Kyoto Protocol and try to reverse the course of events, to cut the CO_2 emissions and to stabilise the situation. The other would be to allow CO_2 emissions to continue unchecked, and to pay the costs of climate change and, in particular, to compensate its victims. Or, more realistically, both these policies must be run in tandem.

This is so because, according to the report, even *stabilised* carbon dioxide levels would lead to a further temperature rise of about 0.4°C, mostly between 2100 and 2200, and push up sea levels by a further eleven to thirty-one inches by 2300 with decreasing rates in later centuries.

Would either of those courses of actions – to cut the emission of greenhouse cases radically, or compensate the victims of global warming – be possible without resorting to a world government?

3. The CFCs example

In the 1970s scientists warned us that the use of chlorofluorocarbons (CFCs) was destroying the ozone layer shielding us from the sun's ultraviolet radiation. Damage to the layer would mean an increase in the incidence of cancer. The observed effects were mainly restricted to the world's southernmost cities, but, in the long run, the entire globe was threatened. Once these putative scientific facts were accepted, resolute international action was taken with the Montreal Protocol in 1985. The industrially developed countries had phased out the use of CFCs by 1999 and the developing countries are now following suit. Could the same happen to the problem with global warming?

It seems that it cannot and the reason is simple: here the costs are considerable, and they are especially high in affluent societies where much of the ordinary lifestyle is built on transport systems emitting CO_2. In particular this is true of the United States. There is a parallel to the Montreal Protocol – the Kyoto Protocol – intended to slow down the CO_2 emissions. However, some nations refuse to take part in the Protocol, particularly the United States which seems adamant in its refusal to join the rest of the world. Peter Singer, in *One World*, quotes President George W. Bush as saying:

> I'll tell you one thing I'm not going to do is I'm not going to let the United States carry the burden for cleaning up the world's air, like the Kyoto treaty would have done. China and India were exempted from that treaty. I think we need to be more even-handed.[5]

It is not difficult for Singer to show that President Bush is being unreasonable. The reason that China and India were exempted is that these are relatively poor countries, who, when their population sizes are taken into account, spread comparatively small amounts of greenhouse gases. The United States, on the other hand, is a rich country producing large amounts of greenhouse gases. As a matter of fact, setting Singapore and some other small, rich countries to one side, the United States produces relatively more greenhouse gases than any other country in the world. Both China and India are below the average. It is clear that if a solution to the problem of global warming is to be sought along the same lines that the world's nations dealt with CFCs then there must be a drastic reduction in the emissions of greenhouse gases by the United States. Any exception for the United States would mean both an injustice and an enormous loss in efficiency. But will it take place? It is hard to believe that it will. Even if, after the publication of the *Fourth Assessment Report* on global warming, the Bush administration has been on the defensive, it rejects mandatory caps on carbon dioxide emissions.

It is noteworthy that even an advanced country like Sweden is highly refractory in this respect. The Swedish Prime Minister, Fredrik Reinfeldt, has famously claimed that Sweden has been so successful in its attempt to restrict emissions of greenhouse gases, that it would not be cost-effective to invest more resources in this respect.[6] What, then, are the facts about Sweden? The official picture is that there has been a seven per cent cut in emissions between 1990 and 2005. However, the official statistics are misleading. If emissions relating to air and sea transports are included, there has been no cut at all. Moreover, the emission per capita in a country like Sweden is enormous when compared with the situation in the world at large. So a *just* solution, globally speaking, requires *drastic* cuts in an economy such as Sweden's. Sweden is no exception, and as a matter of fact, no rich country in the world can be an exception.

In the United States it is very clear what kind of opposition is triggered by the suggestion that a cap on emissions must be undertaken: the opposition is mainly situated among the owners of the oil industry. We must bear in mind that *both* the major American political parties are deeply dependent on money from the oil industry. The subject has been investigated by the Center for Public Integrity: Investigatory Journalism in the Public Interest. The largest subsidies go to the Republicans, but the Democrats receive their share as well. The report notes:

- The Center found that the industry has spent more than $381 million on lobbying activities since 1998, pushing hard on everything from a new national energy policy to obscure changes in the tax code.
- The industry has given more than $67 million in campaign contributions in federal elections since the 1998 election cycle, about a fifth of the amount it has spent on lobbying.
- Oil and gas companies overwhelmingly favored Republicans over Democrats in their campaign giving, the study found. Just over 73 percent of the industry's campaign contributions have gone to Republican candidates and organizations.[7]

And this is what is said, by the same source, about both parties:

The two national parties each took in more than any individual candidate, national Republican committees getting $24 million and Democrats a bit under $8 million.[8]

It could be argued that unless the United States eventually follows suit along the lines of the Kyoto Protocol, the *citizens* of the United States will themselves have to pay a heavy price. So, at the end of the day, American citizens will push towards a reasonable solution to the problem.

This argument is not entirely correct, however. It may well be that damages to the United States from global warming will be much less than the damage to other parts of the world. There may even be some gains for American citizens from global warming, and, more importantly, in the present context, it seems as though what we are facing is a tragedy of the commons.[9] Most American citizens, just like the Swedes, may prefer a world with little emission of greenhouse gases to a world with large emissions, but, at whatever level of emissions, it may be preferable for people living in the United States, or in Sweden, to continue with their *own* levels of emission. This is definitive of a tragedy of the commons, and it seems to be typical of many global environmental problems.

It could be contended that if no action is taken the future costs will be tremendous, so even if the costs for preventative action are considerable it is better to bear them than to wait for the disaster. One could here point to the so-called Stern report, according to which global warming could shrink the global economy by twenty per cent, while taking action now would cost just one per cent of global gross domestic product. This report has been criticised for being too optimistic, and, even if it is realistic, this does not mean that the tragedy of the commons logic goes away. People generally may now perceive even one per cent as too high a cost. They may feel, correctly, that if they make a sacrifice, nothing good will come from it, since other nations will not follow suit and a feeling of mutual distrust is reinforced.

What about the other putative solution to the problem, then? Could we foresee a situation where the costs of global warming are carried in a just manner, by all states on the globe irrespective of whether they gain or lose from it? This is even more difficult to believe, considering how huge these costs are likely to be, according to the Stern report. Yet it seems to be a great hazard indeed to settle for it. If I were a peasant living in Bangladesh, I would hesitate to place the fate of my children in the hands of affluent people living far away in the hope that they would take care of my children once their land is gone.

4. How would a world government handle global warming?

It is likely that a world government would opt for a compromise position. It would restrict the emission of greenhouse gases in a principled manner that cannot be rejected by reasonable people around the world, irrespective of where they happen to live. There are lots of good suggestions about possible forms the global legislation could take. The most promising idea, it seems to me, is to rely on individual quota. The suggestion has been developed by the well-known ecologist George Monbiot in books and articles, for example, in a brief article written as a response to the Stern report in *The Guardian*. The idea is to decide upon a global cap and then:

> use the cap to set a personal carbon ration. Every citizen is given a free annual quota of carbon dioxide. He or she spends it by buying gas and electricity, petrol and train and plane tickets. If they run out, they must buy the rest from someone who has used less than his or her quota. This accounts for about 40% of the carbon dioxide we produce. The remainder is auctioned off to companies. And the remaining problems would be taken care of by compensatory measures. (*The Guardian*, 31 October 2006)

The world government will still have to struggle for many hundreds of years with the effects of global warming, as we know from the recent reports from the IPCC. However, being sovereign, being able to command resources on a global scale, it is likely that it will also find solutions to pressing problems.

A world government would have several options here, of course. One possibility is to give massive aid to those countries near the ones that have been taken away by rising ocean levels in order to help them make room for the environmental refugees. Another possibility would be to give environmental refugee quotas to all countries in the world, without economic compensation. The important thing, in either case, would be to find a global solution which no one could reasonably reject.

5. Scarce natural resources – one example: oil

There is no denying that oil is a scarce resource. Some say it will be used up sooner rather than later,[10] others claim that it may take a considerable time to reach that point. However, eventually this scarce resource will be used up, or, nearly so (the very last drips may have become so expensive that no one wants to use them). This is a rather standard representation of the present situation:

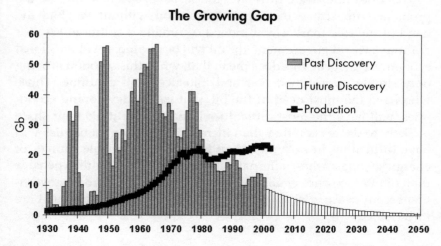

The Growing Gap

Figure 4.1: This figure is from Dr Campbell, a Trustee of the Oil Depletion Analysis Centre (ODAC), a charitable organisation in London that is dedicated to researching the date and impact of the peak and decline of world oil production due to resource constraints and raising awareness of the serious consequences. (http://www.hubbertpeak.com accessed on 1 November 2005.)

But is this really a problem? Will we not be able to find better substitutes for oil? Should we not do so anyway if we want to handle the problem with greenhouse gases? Is it not even *desirable* that we get rid of our dependence upon oil?

I concede that we need to find alternatives to the use of oil. However, this may take some time, and it may be very costly, at least in the beginning. This means that people living in rich countries will be hard put to restrict *their* use. They may be complacent when their governments fight wars over the existing reserves of oil. It is not far-fetched to see the US-led war against Iraq as a fight over existing oil reserves. It is also likely, alas, that much of the French opposition to the US-led war has to do with a competing interest in the same oil reserves. There may be more of the same to come in the future.

There is no doubt that all this creates a rationale for having a world government.

This does not mean, however, that it is *impossible* to handle the problem with scarce resources such as oil without it. Here the hand of the free market will indeed command a solution. With or without a world government, the oil will be phased out of the global economy. However, this does mean that, while this solution is being only slowly approached war and injustices will continue. Those who have the most need of the oil, that is, the developing economies, will have the most difficulties in paying for it. So their share is likely to decrease rather than increase. The same economies will have difficulties in exchanging oil for more sustainable sources of energy so long as these alternative sources are even more expensive than oil. We see once again how the arguments for a world government from peace, global justice and a sustainable environment are intertwined.

6. Scarce resources – a second example: water

A few years ago the United Nations designated 2003 as the International Year of Freshwater. Several reports were published, and the public soon learnt – but has probably since forgotten – that more than half of humanity will be living with water shortages, depleted fisheries and polluted coastlines within fifty years because of a worldwide water crisis. Waste and inadequate management of water are the main culprits behind growing problems, particularly in poverty-ridden regions, says one study, the most comprehensive of its kind. The United Nations Environment Programme, working with more than 200 water resource experts worldwide, produced this report. Based on data from NASA, the World Health Organization and other agencies, the report finds:

- Severe water shortages affecting at least 400 million people today will affect 4 billion people by 2050.
- Adequate sanitation facilities are lacking for 2.4 billion people, about 40% of humankind.

- Half of all coastal regions, where 1 billion people live, have degraded through overdevelopment or pollution.

As water becomes scarce, conflicts over existing resources are to be expected. These are problems that create no media hype, and they are indeed eclipsed by the concern for global warming and yet, setting matters of scale to one side, they are even more *urgent* than the (future) problems created by global warming.

It is an often reported fact that more than a dozen nations receive most of their water from rivers that cross the borders of neighbouring countries viewed as hostile, such as Botswana, Bulgaria, Cambodia, the Congo, Gambia, the Sudan and Syria, all receiving seventy-five per cent or more of their fresh water from the river flow of often hostile upstream neighbours. In the Middle East, a region marked by hostility between nations, obtaining adequate water supplies is a high political priority. For example, water has been a contentious issue in negotiations between Israel and Syria. In recent years, Iraq, Syria and Turkey have exchanged verbal threats over their use of shared rivers.[11]

Of course, water is different from oil. There is no way of phasing water out of the global economy. The problem is to find the means to a sustainable use of water. How could this be done? Can it be done, with or without a world government?

The ideas about how the crisis should be met are varied. Some suggest a merely technological solution, desalination. Here Saudi Arabia, Israel and Japan are in the lead. There are approximately 11,000 desalination plants in 120 nations in the world, sixty per cent of them in the Middle East.[12] Others argue that a market approach to water management would help to resolve the situation, which can be seen as a case of the tragedy of the commons. For example, the Harvard Middle East Water Project wants to assign a value to water, rather than treat rivers and streams as some kind of free natural commodity like air. Other strategies to confront the growing global water problem include slowing population growth, reducing pollution, better management of present supply and demand and water conservation.

This is not the place to assess these various different proposals. But I think all will agree that both the first and the third strategies are easily seen as complementary, rather than as alternatives to one another. The second, market solution, is highly controversial, of course. When it has been attempted in poor countries, such as Bolivia, the result has been disastrous, because of the socio-political consequences of the approach.

Will the problem of scarce water supplies be solved without a world government? This is likely, if it is solved at all. The reason is that many of the keys to a solution are, after all, national. However, there are some aspects of the problem that are truly global. These are the problems that have to do with pollution. In this context, it would be helpful to have access to global decisions, based on fair ratios for the spread of all sorts of substances that can cause harm in the long run. Note also that, unless the problems to do with scarcity of water are handled on a global political level, the competition over scarce resources is likely to engender war and civil disorder in many places around the world.

7. Endangered species

It is now part of received wisdom that every day between thirty-five and 150 species of life become extinct. Does it matter? If it matters, to whom does it matter?

First, there are deep ecologists, who believe that a rich variation of species, or a conservation of existing species, is of value in its own right.[13] This is a highly controversial view, of course. Personally, I believe that it is false. Secondly, there is no denying that when some species become extinct, this means a loss to human beings. This is most obviously so when species from which we feed become extinct. The World Bank report on the water situation looked also at global problems of oceans and seas:

- Coral reefs, mangrove forests and sea grass beds, important grounds for young fish and for environmental needs, face threats from over fishing, development and pollution.

- Oxygen-depleted seas, caused by industrial and agricultural runoff, could lead to fishery collapses and 'dead zones' in such places as the Gulf of Mexico.
- Wild fish catches are levelling off worldwide. With 75% of fish stocks fully exploited, fleets have turned to fish lower on ocean food chains. Ecologists worry that entire fisheries will collapse as these 'junk fish' are used up. Increased demand for fish is being made up through aquaculture, which brings other environmental concerns.

Moreover, the very existence of a rich and varied nature has, to many people, an aesthetic value. They take pleasure in nature, and this source of pleasure seems to be, to many, an extremely important one. For this reason too, it might be a good idea to save the mangrove forests. Finally, when a species becomes extinct, this means that no members of that species will exist any more. To the extent that these individuals would have been sentient beings, it makes good sense to say that their absence means a loss. This is not a loss that is felt by anyone in particular, but it is a loss in the sense that the world is a worse place without those individuals than it would have been with them around.

If some of this is accepted, if at least it is accepted that it is a bad thing when fish upon which human beings feed become extinct, then there is a place for concern. How can we save coral reefs and sea grass beds, how can we best meet threats from over fishing and pollution, how can we repair oxygen-depleted seas? The problem is – as was the case with global warming and greenhouse gases – that some nations are economically strongly dependent on practices that are raising global concerns, such as over fishing or the destruction of mangrove forests. These nations share the interest held by the rest of the world population in a world without ecological problems, but what we are facing once again is a tragedy of the commons; they would prefer a world without ecological problems to a world with ecological problems, but, given the situation as it is, irrespective of how it happens to be, they have good egoistical reasons for carrying on with their practices. The harm they do globally, by sticking to their bad practices, is less, when assessed from their egoistical point of view, than the gain they make assessed in the same manner.

It is with reference to this kind of mechanism that we can explain a statement such as the one made by Masayuki Komatsu, a senior Fisheries Agency official and a long-term delegate to the annual meetings of the International Whaling Commission ('IWC') on 15 September 2004: 'Eating whale is a key part of Japanese culture'.[14] Of course, a possible solution, in principle, would be to *pay* these nations for not destroying nature, to *bribe* them into a better behaviour.

There are two main problems with such a strategy, however. First, it would be extremely difficult to find public support for subsidies of this kind among the world populations. For individual governments to have their populations accepting taxes designed to bribe certain nations into better behaviour would certainly be met with much dismay. Secondly, it would be tempting for some governments to find excuses for not being among the nations that provide a net payment to this effect.

Could not economic sanctions do the trick, then? Could not the nations that do not take part in over fishing or the destruction of the mangrove forests, say, threaten the nations that do with heavy economic sanctions? We know how difficult it is to make international sanctions stick, even in cases where they seem to be warranted for strictly humanitarian reasons. And it is a problem that while some nations behave badly in one respect, others behave badly in another respect, so if the problem should be dealt with successfully through economic sanctions, then the very same nation that is subjected to (some) sanctions would take part in meting out (other) sanctions against other nations. Such a system stretches credulity.

A world government, however, could *force* recalcitrant states to abstain from their, from an ecological point of view, irresponsible behaviour.

8. Conclusion

It is hard to deny that the solution to some environmental problems such as global warming requires a world government. It is less obvious that problems to do with scarce resources such as oil and water cannot be solved without our resorting to a world government. However, unless problems to do with scarce resources are approached on a global political level, through one sovereign political agent, it is likely that many of the other known global problems, to do with war and injustice, will grow even more acute. So there seem to be *indirect* reasons with reference to scarce resources such as oil and water to resort to a world government.

It might also be wise to add the following. Only a few years ago, few of us knew anything about global warming. Now everyone is discussing it. It seems to provide a perfect rationale for world government. It is highly likely that other environmental challenges, that for the moment we know nothing about, will rise on the horizon. Some of them may well, for all we know, come to eclipse the problem of global warming. So there are good reasons also to try to prepare for the unexpected. Also there is no denying that some future environmental threats and challenges might be of such an order that they cannot successfully be handled unless they are addressed on a global scale.

It is wise, therefore, to opt for a world government also since, for environmental reasons, we *may* come to need it in the future.

5
Democracy

1. Introduction

U nless we succeed in establishing a world government, we are not likely to obtain perpetual peace, global justice or a good environment, but this does not settle the question of whether we ought to strive for a world government. The project may be hopelessly utopian (unrealistic), or, even if realistic, it may be problematic in itself. So perhaps war, injustice and environmental problems are things with which we have to bear for the foreseeable future. Let us, however, assume that a world government is both realistic and desirable as such, as will be argued in the following chapters. What shape should it take?

Among the advocates of a world government, some have been of a rather elitist bent – H. G. Wells being the best-known one. The establishment of an elitist world government seems unlikely unless it is brought about through violent conquest of the rest of the world by a superpower. This has not really happened since the rise of the Roman Empire, even if Napoleon, British imperialists, Hitler and others did attempt to follow suit, so it is not likely that it will happen in the foreseeable future. Moreover, it seems obvious to me that an elitist world government is hardly desirable in itself. For these reasons, I will not discuss this possibility any further. I will take for granted that the world government could and should be democratic. My interest, then, is in global democracy.

Democracy, however, takes many different forms, some rather elitist, others rather populist, so we need to discuss the most important alternatives here. Provided a world government is a realistic and desirable goal in the first place, what *kind* of global democracy should be established? How should this question be answered? With reference to what kind of evidence should an answer be provided? This is not merely a matter of going for something that suits our personal taste. We need a notion of democracy which satisfies two important desiderata. First, it should be such that the idea of a global democracy becomes as realistic as possible. It must be 'realistic' in the sense that the idea of such a global democracy could command strong popular support all over the world, rendering its establishment possible through democratic means. Secondly, it should be such that, once in place, the world government will function as efficiently as possible. Its efficiency should be judged in relation to the problems it is intended to solve: to guarantee perpetual peace; global justice; and a good environment.

Are these two requirements at odds with one another? So it may seem, and unless appearances are deceptive, we are in deep trouble. However, I will try to show that that appearances *are* deceptive; that the two requirements do go well together. There is one *unique* view of democracy that best suits *both* of them.

2. Ideals of democracy – populist democracy

We need an ideal of democracy which renders it possible for us to assess to what degree a world government serving a sovereign world parliament could be democratic. I will begin my discussion by stating my own favoured ideal and then go on to compare it with possible rival ideals.

In the present context democracy will be conceived of as a method of collective decision making. A collective decision D, is reached by a collectivity C in a democratic manner, if, and only if, D is reached through a method guaranteeing that the will of the members of C prevail. If there is no unanimous will among the members of C, but if a will of a unique majority should exist, then it is crucial that the method guarantees that the will of this majority should prevail. If there is no unique majority, since there are more than two ways to solve the matter, and there are cyclical majorities, in a way to be explained, then the exact outcome of the decision is not crucial to its democratic status – as long as one of the alternatives in the top cycle is picked.

When I speak of cycles I think of situations such as the following – and here I simplify by discussing a situation where there exists just *one* cycle. Three alternatives have been presented, X, Y and Z. One third of the demos prefer X to Y and Y to Z. Another third of the demos prefer Y to Z and Z to X. A final third of the demos prefer Z to X and X to Y. If you think about the situation you find that there is no unique majority here. X wins over Y, and Y wins over Z, while Z wins over X – if you take a vote and allow the majority in each case to decide.

Here my idea is to allow someone, the chairperson, say, to choose. And, likewise, if there are only two options but a draw, the outcome doesn't matter to the democratic status of the decision. It can be selected at random or by a dictator – with respect to this decision – such as a chairperson. In these cases, the crucial thing is that the method used (a random procedure or a dictator) to reach the decision is such that, *had* there been a unique majority will, then this unique majority will *would* have prevailed.[1]

Note that my point is not that there is something wrong with Arrow's well-known theorem showing that no social welfare function can satisfy all his demands.[2] The collective decision method I advocate is clearly at variance with the idea that there should be no dictator. But in situations where there is no unique majority, I do not find it problematic to accept that a dictator (a chairperson, or a random mechanism) decides among the alternatives in the (top) cycle.

Clearly, this is a descriptive understanding of democracy. No evaluations need to be made when we want to settle whether a certain decision has been arrived at in a democratic manner. I see this as a positive. Moreover, there is no restriction as to which collectivities

Democracy

can take democratic decisions about what. I see this too as positive.

There are some vague notions employed in the definition. In particular, it is far from clear what it means to say that something is in accordance with the 'will' of an individual or a collectivity. The core notion here is that of a will of an individual. The will of the majority (or a minority, or any other group) is a function of the will of the individuals who make it up. However, what does it mean for an individual to 'will' that a task be solved one way rather than another?

Since our interest in the idea is political, I think it reasonable to take the will of a person to be tantamount to some kind of properly and explicitly expressed opinion. We are not interested here in interests, or welfare, or anything of the kind (as we may be in moral philosophy or welfare economics). Here we focus on what people themselves have to say about the possible solution to a certain problem. The reason why a certain individual, taking part in democratic decision making, wants a certain matter to be solved in one way rather than another may well be tactical; log-rolling is an acceptable and standard part of much democratic decision making.

I take it for granted that there is a way for people to express, in the relevant way, their political opinions. It should be *possible* for them to do so; no one should have manipulated the voting machine, if such a machine is used, for example. However, those who press the wrong button are themselves to blame; their mistaken vote *is* an expression of their 'will' – in the relevant sense of the word. All this means that, in order for there to be a democratic decision in the first place, there must exist political agents prepared to voice their opinions (in an appropriate manner).

Once democracy has been defined in this strictly naturalistic manner (without having recourse to any value terms in the definiens), it is possible to articulate various different ideals in terms of democracy. Most political ideologies have something to say about democracy, and most present-day political ideologies are in one way or another favourable to democracy. In each political ideology there is some room for democratic decision making. If the understanding of democracy here defined is used in the statement of such ideologies,

71

then it is possible to specify such things as what decisions should, and what decisions should not, according to a certain political ideology, be taken in a democratic manner. Moreover, with respect to those that should be taken in a democratic manner, according to the political ideology in question, it is also possible to specify by whom they should be taken.

It is important to note that all plausible ideals of democracy leave some room, not only for democratic decision making, but also for dictatorship.[3] I have already noted that a chairperson may sometimes, in the case of ties, work as a dictator when political decisions are reached. Even more importantly, individuals must be allowed to act with respect to themselves and their personal belongings as dictators – within limits set by decency, morality and the law. This causes a problem for the so-called all-affected principle in politics. Even if my decisions affect other people I should be allowed to take them all by myself. In all democracies the voters should be allowed to decide for themselves how to vote. It doesn't make sense, then, to claim that everyone who is affected by a decision should have a say in it. I will return to this problem in a later chapter on the implementation of global democracy. It should be noted that on this conception of democracy there may exist many and rather different *mechanisms* for arriving at democratic decisions. The crucial thing is that the method used guarantees that, if there is a unique will of the people, then this will is going to prevail.

The most obvious way of seeing to this is perhaps to meet 'under the oaks' (to use Rousseau's way of putting it), to have everybody putting forward his or her proposals, to have a public discussion about them, and then take a vote where the majority, if a unique majority exists, will have its way. This, of course, is the 'classical', 'direct', or 'participatory' technique. Other methods also exist, the most important among them being the 'representative' model.

The rationale behind a system where representatives of a group gather, put forward proposals, discuss them and have a vote is the idea that the decision these people reach is the one those who are represented *would* have reached, had they been able to gather in the same manner. The most effective way of approximating to this (populist) ideal is probably to take a statistical sample of the group in question and allow it to decide matters. This method is rarely used, however (even if small-scale social experiments along this line have been carried out the last decades). The reason that this method is rarely used, I think, is that people are sceptical of such a radical democratic approach. Most people seem to be in favour of democracy only if the ideal is somewhat tempered with a kind of elitism. This is why political parties exist, why people can take up a political career and so forth. A typical representative of this kind of moderate elitism is James Madison, who argued that the elected representatives are likely to be competent and capable of 'discerning the true interest of their country',[4] while those represented were considered to be intolerant, unreliable and unjust. However, a straightforward defence of the populist ideal was given by John Adams, who argued that a representative legislature 'should be an exact portrait, in miniature, of the people at large, as it should think, feel, reason and act like them'.[5] It is noteworthy that, even if there is nothing at all to Madison's scepticism with respect to those who are represented, in a representative democracy there may well exist, in political opinions, a considerable gap between those who are represented and their representatives.

There are two main reasons why, even if those who are represented are *as* competent as their representatives, such a gap may develop. Even if they could do so, those who are represented need not *bother* to form any opinion at all with respect to some political questions (apathy). Or, they may hold opinions that, *if* they bothered to discuss them with others and put them up to critical scrutiny in the manner their representatives do, they would change.

It is debatable whether a representative system based on parties really approaches the populist ideal, but I will not pursue this theme in the present context. I will assume that such a system, especially if the method used to assemble the representatives is strictly proportional and hence allows the various different parties to be represented in a way that is similar to how the preferences are distributed within the electorate, is close enough to the mark to earn the right to be called 'democratic'. When such an assembly takes a decision on behalf of the electorate we are allowed to say that it approximates to the decision the electorate would have taken, had it itself been able to gather, discuss and take a vote. So, in a figurative manner of speaking we may say that it is the electorate who takes the decision, *through* its representatives.

Now, the kind of global democracy I will be defending can be described with reference to this populist ideal of democracy. I believe that it is crucial that a directly elected world parliament be established, and I think it is crucial that this global parliament is sovereign when it comes to adopting laws. Furthermore, it should elect a world government. We are then allowed to say that, again in a figurative manner of speaking, it is the world population who, through their representatives, legislate for themselves and elect their own government.

All this is consistent with the continued existence of nation-states having, from the world parliament, all sorts of political objectives delegated to them, but it does mean that nation-states would lose all their sovereignty. They would be relegated to the role that munici-palities or regions play within nation-states as we *now* know them.

This concession to the nation-state is, however, consistent with the claim that in addition to former nation-states, now relegated to the status of local constituencies, we may need new constituencies as well, on a lower level than the global one. Many contemporary so-called cosmopolitan thinkers such as, for example, David Held, have stressed this point. In Chapter 7 I will discuss and repudiate his suggestion that the introduction of such constituencies should be seen as an alternative to global democracy proper, but there might still be some truth in this position if we see it as a compli-ment rather than as an alternative to global democracy. Still, on the model advocated in this book, the world government would be sovereign in its decisions about which level a certain decision belongs; to the global one, to a national one, or to a transnational one, designed intentionally for the handling of the kind of problem in question.

3. *Ideals of democracy: elitism*

The representative political system should not be conflated with
another technique for reaching collective decisions, which has also
been called 'democratic', but where I find it less clear that it really is
close enough to the mark to earn the right to be so-called. I think here
of a system where no attempt is made to have any will of the people
prevail; the idea is simply that those who rule the people acquire
their mandate in a certain way: through a competitive struggle for
the people's vote. Such a system is 'democratic' according to Joseph
Schumpeter's influential definition of democracy where, 'The
democratic method is that institutional arrangement for arriving
at political decisions in which individuals acquire the power to
decide by means of a competing struggle for the people's vote.'[6]
Political systems satisfying Schumpeter's requirement, but not the
requirements articulated by me, are typically systems where only
two major parties compete. A method of approaching such a system
is, of course, to have a majoritarian election method. For a political
system to have any chance of meeting the strong (classical, populist)
requirements articulated by me it needs to rely on many parties and
a way of achieving such a system is to have a strictly proportionate
electoral system.

It should be noted that, in a representative democracy of the kind
here described, the electorate decides political matters democratically *through* their representatives. However, their *choice* of representatives is not democratic. In a representative system, a delegate,
who is disliked by a majority, may well come to be elected. He or she
is then elected as a representative of a certain minority. According
to Schumpeter's ideal of democracy, the choice of leaders is
'democratic', in my sense of the word, but the subsequent decisions
taken by political leaders cannot be seen even figuratively speaking
as being taken by the people, through them. On the contrary, once
in place they *rule* the people.

We may abide by Schumpeter's advice, of course, and conceive of
democracy without connecting it in any way to the idea that democracy means that the will of (the majority) of those who take collec-

tive decisions prevail. This is just an ideal that is different from the populist one. And there is one aspect of Schumpeter's ideal, where decisions are taken in a 'democratic' manner, as I use the term. Think of the elections where the political leaders are adopted. So my point is not that Schumpeter's ideal is not a democratic one; there is a (restricted) place for democracy in his ideal too. I do believe, however, that in the present context his ideal is inferior to the populist one, and I will try to explain why.

The ambitious claim I'm going to make is that a world parliament should indeed aspire to the populist type of democracy here defined. Only such a system can gain strong global support, and such a system is best suited to its task, that is, to deal with problems to do with peace, justice and a good environment. These are strong claims, of course, and I will do my best to defend them. First an aside, however, on a third ideal of democracy: the deliberative one.

4. Ideals of democracy: deliberative democracy

Since the last time I wrote about the subject (*Populist Democracy. A Defence*, 1992) the notion of *deliberative* democracy has been the focus of much discussion. Here is a representative statement of what has been conceived of as a recent trend:

> Around 1990 the theory of democracy took a definite deliberative turn. Prior to that turn, the democratic ideal was seen mainly in terms of aggregation of preferences or interests into collective decisions through devices such as voting and representation. Under deliberative democracy, the essence of democratic legitimacy should be sought instead in the ability of all individuals subject to a collective decision to engage in authentic deliberation about that decision. These individuals should accept the decision only if it could be justified to them in convincing terms.[7]

Does deliberative democracy present an interesting alternative to more traditional notions of democracy, of importance in the discussion about global democracy?

I think not. On the most charitable interpretation of the above quotation it allows us to conceive of 'deliberative' democracy as a *kind* of (populist) democracy, as here defined. What characterises deliberative democracy, then, is that the members of a collectivity who reach a democratic decision have the possibility of exchanging views in a certain manner, where the result is also, perhaps, that the decision gains a kind of 'legitimacy'. Or, the deliberation among those represented (in a representative democracy) may be seen as a means of lessening the opinion gap between representatives and those represented (commented upon above).

Here new media have been said to be of special interest. I am somewhat sceptical with respect to the possibility that internet communication should be seen as a good means to enlightened discussions between people with different world views. Rather than engendering rational discussions between people of different opinions, the various internet groups that arise spontaneously seem each to engage people who all hold the *same* views on a matter.[8] I may be wrong about this, and if I am, this is good news for democracy in our modern times, but I will not rely in my argument on any optimistic assumptions to this effect.[9]

However, even if in many cases the internet is not a means to enhanced political decision making, it could still be looked upon with sympathy. For the existence of the internet means that now it is easy to mould and organise opinions, in and between political parties and across national borders, to prepare ordinary political manifestations and to put new political questions on the agenda. An initiative such as the one urging that a parliamentary assembly should be added to the United Nations would hardly have been so successful if it had not been based on the internet.[10] So new media are after all helpful to the global political cause.

Having said this about new media, such as the internet, let me now return to the quoted passage about deliberative democracy. On a less charitable interpretation of it, the point in discussing deliberative democracy is to put forward a *competing* notion or ideal of democracy, according to which a collective decision is democratic once it has been preceded by a certain discourse, or once it is in fact accepted by those concerned by it as reasonable, *irrespective of how it was reached*. What gives this impression is the fact that the author goes on to assert that there are two closely connected recent ideas of democracy, the 'deliberative' and the 'discursive', and that they have one thing in common: 'they share some key features, including a rejection of aggregative models of democracy'.[11] However, although such an interpretation leaves me unsatisfied, I will not enter further into exegesis. It must suffice to note that, on my account of democracy, be it deliberative or not, it *is* a method of aggregation of political preferences. I will count neither Schumpeter's notion nor any deliberative notion inconsistent with the one I have here defined as an adequate (for my purposes) notion of democracy. Not even a combination of Schumpeter's approach and the deliberative one (where a world government earns its right to rule through a competitive struggle for the people's vote and where there is a worldwide political discourse going on) is enough to satisfy my radical demands. In order to meet my demands a world parliament legislating for the world must be responsive to the will of the people of the world. The global constitution should take such a shape that it makes sense to claim that the world population, through the world parliament, legislate for themselves and select their own government.

5. The case for the populist ideal of global democracy

My use of the word democracy along the lines given above is, of course, the result of an assumption on my part. However, this is an assumption which is fruitful to the purposes of the present discussion. I use it to state my populist ideal of global democracy. I think of global democracy as global populist democracy. My query, in the present context, is if there is a place for 'democratic' rule in this sense, in a society where citizenship has become cosmopolitan, then I submit that a populist ideal of global democracy satisfies the two requirements given above. Nothing less radical than a populist global democracy would be considered worth striving for, so nothing short of a populist global democracy is realistic, in particular if we think that it should be established through democratic means. This claim is perhaps not very controversial. The next claim is controversial, however. I also argue that nothing less radical than a populist global democracy is likely to solve those problems on which it should focus. The argument is as follows.

First, we should note that when the claim is made that democratic decision making should be resorted to in some instances there are two main arguments that are usually put forward to substantiate this. One is that in a situation where many people are affected by a decision it is important to find a method of solving conflicts, which means that all *interests* are aggregated in a fair manner. Democratic decision making can be a means to approximate this ideal, at least if we are allowed to assume that the individuals are *rational and egoistically motivated*. Everyone is allowed to live out his or her egoism, and the decision method is thought to work in such a manner that the resulting distribution of resources is, with respect to the interests of the citizens, just, or, at least, not too unjust. We may speak here of an aggregation of interests model of democracy. And something that is helpful in a democracy to the establishment of a fair outcome, is the so-called median voter theorem proved by Duncan Black in 1948.[12] There is no need here to go into technical details, but the theorem means, very roughly that, if people compete in a democracy for the tax rate they see as most favourable to them individually, then the (median) person who has equally many people who are poorer than him and many people who are richer will have his way – we assume here that the poorer you are, the higher tax rate you want. Now, since the median person is typically less well to do than the person with average income, this means that (populist) democracy has a built in tendency towards economic equality.

The other argument is epistemic. It is argued with reference to what has been known as Condorcet's Jury theorem that majority decision making may be a way of finding the *right* decision. The thrust of the theorem is the observation that, if a group of people try to find the correct solution to a problem impartially then, on average, they will be right more often than not, so the probability that a decision reached through the majority principle will be right is higher than the probability that a decision reached by any individual would be right. The more people who act independently of one another the higher the probability. [13] So it might be a good idea to have the decision reached democratically.

In real political situations both these motives are often mixed; the motives are mixed both behind the establishment of democratic institutions in the first place and behind the assumptions of the actual political behaviour of citizens. We need *sound* decisions resulting in a cake that we can divide among ourselves, and then a *fair* solution when the cake is divided among us.

There is, however, an important asymmetry here. If we establish democracy in order to achieve a fair distribution with respect to the interests of the citizens, and allow each citizen to vote in order to promote his or her own interests, it does not matter if some, instead, cast their votes according to what they take to be the *common* good. If they are reasonably successful in their predictions there is no distortion of the result.

However, if we establish democracy in order to ascertain a *correct* solution to a problem, and those who vote do not *aim* at the common good, then we are in deep trouble. Condorcet's theorem then doesn't apply, or it applies only in its converse and perverse form: if most people are wrong most of the time then the probability that the majority are wrong is even higher than the probability that an individual is wrong. This may well be a fact where people do not even *aim* at the common good.

I suppose that when a parliament is elected on a national level we try to see to it both that different interests are respected, but also that many points of view will each have a voice. The parliament is supposed to guarantee that there is no oppression of the majority by the minority. Through the democratic arrangements the median voter is given a privileged position. Then there is a government and other special agencies which take political action. We want them to take their decisions in a democratic manner. We want them to arrive at the *right* decision. Here the epistemic argument is operative.

There are many problems relating to the aggregation of interest model of democracy. One may think that, in order for it to work perfectly, one should give different votes to different people in relation to each political decision; those with bigger stakes in an issue should have more votes.[14] Or, we may seek a way of forcing people to reach unanimous decisions.[15] The assumption then is that those for whom more is at stake will hold out longer than those for whom less is at stake. But proportionate influence is difficult to accomplish, at least in a fair manner that would receive general acceptance, so in most circumstances we have to stay satisfied with the *all affected view*, that is, with the view that all who are affected by the decision should have a vote (and have only one vote). This is at least a means of rendering it more difficult for a minority to suppress the majority – which does not mean that such suppression is impossible, of course.[16] None the less this must then mean that there is a constant fear that the majority will suppress some minorities. So when democracy is established the problems of the minorities must somehow be managed, and the usual idea here is to rely on *education* of some kind. The majority need to be educated into understanding the special needs of all sorts of minorities. Then it is helpful to have a proportionate electoral system, where minorities at least stand a *chance* of entering the parliament.

The problems connected with the epistemic model of democracy are no less acute, of course. How can a situation be established where people are prepared to cast their votes for the common good, rather than their own good? How can we find methods of education ascertaining that the average person is, on average, right more often than wrong when he or she makes up his or her mind? However, since political democracy in modern society is rarely direct, the epistemic model is, from a political point of view, of interest mainly where political assemblies, such as parliaments and governments in particular reach their decisions.

I will not go into the general problems with the two models of democracy in the present context. When we are discussing the problem of a world parliament intended to solve global problems to do with peace, justice and the environment I think the prospects of fulfilling the aims of both the interest aggregation model and the epistemic model are very good indeed. This is so, at least, if we assume that the world government will stick to its task and not try to meddle with problems that should not be in its remit to solve, but left to other political authorities further down in the hierarchy. In this chapter I will simply make the assumption that a world government does stick to its task. In a later chapter I will try to defend why this is a reasonable assumption to make.

Given this assumption, let us first consider the epistemic model. I have argued in preceding chapters that the role of the world government is not to solve problems to do with global injustice through redistribution between individuals on the globe. This would mean that on a global scale we would have had to rely heavily on the aggregation of interests model of democracy. This may indeed seem problematic. However, for reasons already given, and for reasons to be given in chapters to come, it is neither feasible nor desirable to obtain this kind of redistribution. The problems with global injustices should rather be confronted through global legislation of various kinds, ensuring that those who are poor will be empowered, and hence capable of bettering their position themselves. Suppose this is how the problem is dealt with, then it is mainly a matter of finding the most efficient means to this end, which should be the focus of a world parliament when it adopts new laws. The same is true of problems to do with the environment. Here reasonable quotas and general restrictions on the use of scarce resources or dangerous materials should be designed, and the problem, once again, is to find the best solutions to the problems.

This is even more true of world policing missions when civil war threatens somewhere on the globe. So, on the whole, a world parliament and a world government, will, much more than national parliaments and national governments, have to solve problems where there would be little controversy over what a satisfactory solution would amount to. However, there is no denying that decisions to do with peace, justice and the environment may sometimes be burdensome, and, particularly in respect to the environment, they may affect people differently. Some will have to bear *extra* burdens, either because they are rich and have to give away much or, because they are poor and cannot compensate for this by accessing scarce resources in the way that those who are rich did in the past. Here is where we must rely on the aggregation of interest model of democracy. By having a world parliament representative of the entire population of the world we will have a means to guarantee that at least no elite will be able to suppress the masses. At the same time it must be noted that the system does not guarantee that the interests of some important minorities will not be set to one side. One may think here, for example, of aboriginal populations who rely crucially on resources which the rest of the global population want desperately to rescue.

6. Global political parties

All this means that, while global democracy requires a global political culture and, preferably, global political parties, this culture need not be all-encompassing. This culture should concern itself with problems to do with peace, international justice and the environment. The parties ought to try to devise effective solutions to these problems. There is no doubt that many conflicting and inconsistent proposals will be put forward, and political parties can be arranged around these. The nation-states, robbed of their sovereignty but still existing, can in most cases be natural constituencies, although some nation-states will be too small to this effect. There may also be parties organising groups such as aboriginal peoples that are not entirely global, but neither altogether national in their orientation. Such parties may present a special view to the world parliament on, say, ecological problems. If they succeed in entering the world parliament, then this may enable them to safeguard their interests. There is no guarantee that they will succeed, of course, either in entering the parliament or, once they are there, in convincing the majority that they are right.

It is also to be expected that, when global parties dedicated to global problems develop, traditional national parties will not just abdicate from the scene. They will also take part in the global discussion and, in competition with global parties, present candidates in the elections. I speculate, however, that they will not be entirely successful and global parties will eventually gain ground. However, the outcome here is not crucial to the success of the idea of global democracy. The crucial thing is that the delegates elected to the world parliament are elected on a global political programme.

There is *some* room for the aggregation of interest model of democracy on a global level as well. Decisions taken by the world parliament and the world government in order to safeguard peace, international justice and a good environment will often, as we have seen, impose at least short-term costs on the citizens of the world. It is important that these costs are spread in a fair manner. To this effect, it is important that the world parliament is representative of the entire population of the globe and it is crucial, in particular, that the majority of citizens in the world, who are relatively poor are correctly represented in order to avoid the possibility that a rich minority will be capable of shifting the main burdens onto those who are poor.

Now, since putting the burdens mainly on the shoulders of those who are poor would be unfair, those who are poor will have both egoistic and moral reasons that they can appeal to when they protest against such proposals, so it is hard to believe that a global democracy would not work to their advantage (and towards a less unjust situation in the world at large). The median voter in the world population is relatively and absolutely speaking a poor person.

As has been noted, however, there exists a risk that some *minorities* will be dealt harshly with, and, of course, this risk, which exists in any political system, is exacerbated if the global political authorities do not restrict themselves to the problems to which they *should* restrict themselves. I leave a discussion of this problem for a later chapter, however, where it can be confronted in a less abstract and speculative manner (after having presented a realistic road map towards the establishment of global democracy).

7. Is there a case for elitism?

It seems, then, that a radical, populist version of democracy would suit our global needs. But could we not rest satisfied with something less radical, such as a Schumpeter version of democracy? Would it not work just as well?

I cannot see that it would be desirable to establish it, even if it were possible, for this is a highly elitist notion of democracy. It is true that, if the world's population were allowed, directly or, more plausibly indirectly, to elect, re-elect or dismiss the world government, this would mean that, if the incumbent world government did not make the kind of decisions most people would want it to make, a majority of the global population could get rid of it. However, unless there is a representative system, allowing a majority also to have a say on *politics*, the risk is obvious that, when one government gets exchanged for another, the other government will be no more liked than the first one. As a matter of fact, from a political point of view, they may be almost indistinguishable, like the Republicans and the Democrats in the United States. A likely result would be global political apathy, of the kind we find in the United States but not, for example, in the Scandinavian countries, where the populist ideal of democracy is adhered to. We would find a decline in *de facto* authority of the global political system, and political decisions taken that are not to the advantage of those who are worst off, but to the advantage of the global political and economic elite.

Note that, in at least a figurative manner of speaking, a representative model allowing the world population through their representatives to legislate for themselves, allows a kind of political participation. This will be most clear to those who are members of global parties, but it will make sense for anyone who just sympathises with a party, and who has cast his or her vote for a candidate from this party to say, when a certain bill is passed in the world parliament 'we won', or, 'we failed, so we have to continue with our argumentation and campaigns'. If, instead, we have leaders who enact *for* us, we do not participate. We can like or dislike the bills and laws they allow to pass, of course, but we cannot think of this in terms of success and failure.

It is, therefore, hard to believe that a global democracy, modelled on Schumpeter's ideas, would command much enthusiasm among people at large. Also it is no easy task to establish global democracy in the first place. So it is difficult to believe that *such* a global democracy will ever see the light of the day.

Schumpeter's notion of democracy doesn't seem capable of handling pressing global problems, then. It invites a situation where an elite will rule the world in accordance with their own private vested interests, or at least, it invites the *suspicion* that this might happen. Finally, it does not involve the global population in global political problems. So if we are to believe in global democracy, we should invest our hopes in a radical, populist understanding of democracy.

Is the populist ideal utopian? It is not. At least not if understood as I have laid out in the present context. It is realised, to an acceptable degree, in many European democracies. So why should it not be possible to realise it on a global level?

I have met the objection that this is a matter of scale. In big countries such as the United States populist democracy is not feasible; here we have to rely on rule by an elite. But I don't think that the diagnosis is correct. The crucial factor seems to be political culture and the electoral system used, rather than scales. Even in large countries, where the political culture is favourable to populist democracy and, in particular, where the electoral system is proportionate, we should expect populist democracy to flourish. In Germany, for example, we have a large nation-state practising populist democracy. Here political ideologies and political parties, rather than persons, seem to matter. We know this also from other European countries.

However, there may be a special difficulty in countries with many nationalities, and if this is so, it means that there would be a problem for global democracy, of course. Kai Nielsen has put forward this objection in correspondence:

> Our nation-states are run (governed would be a more neutral term) by elites and where there are multi-national nation-states, particularly when they are multi-linguistic (Canada, Finland, Belgium, Spain, South Africa, New Zealand, India, Indonesia, China) this problem of elites is made almost unsolvable for we could not have popular democracy there for only elites would

have the linguistic skills to function effectively in parliament. Would this not be greatly exacerbated in the world parliament? We cannot in Canada or South Africa have a politics in the vernacular, as Will Kymlicka puts it, and that looks like a necessary condition for a popular democracy.

I tend to be more optimistic. My conjecture is that the problems in the United States and Canada with obtaining populist democracy has more to do with political traditions and electoral systems. It is noteworthy that in Switzerland, clearly a multi-national and multi-linguistic state, a highly populist version of democracy is practised, with many parties, each gaining support from different ethnic groups, and with recourse in many cases to popular referenda. Furthermore, even if there are tensions in a country like Spain, there are still political parties operating at a national level, having a say also in the Basque country and in Catalonia, since *many* people there support them; in Finland, moreover, *most* people in the Swedish-speaking minority are organised in the traditional Finnish parties.

Nielsen himself doesn't draw the conclusion that global democracy is impossible. Instead he opts for elitism:

> I would bite the bullet and say that in our nation-states we have rule by elites and it would be no worse (and perhaps better) with a world government. Sadly, it seems that popular democracy is only possible in unilingual (usually small) nation-states like Iceland.

Having argued repeatedly that global elitist democracy is not *feasible*, I cannot take a similar tack. I admit, however, that in different parts of the world, because of different political traditions representatives to the world parliament may come to be elected in very different manners, and on many different grounds. But if I am right in saying that the populist model of democracy has advantages, not only in that it can motivate people to take part in the political process, but also in that it provides for efficient rule by the people, I think the odds that it will spread globally are good. Unless it does, however, I submit that there will be no global democracy in the first place.

8. Should a populist democracy be tempered with a system of judicial review?

I have met the objection that democracy is not always the most efficient tool if we want to deal with problems to do with oppression. Democracy needs to be tempered with a system of judicial review:

> The track record of democratic institutions as means to deal effectively with *any* important areas of public policy (whether domestic or global) is patchy at best. To take just one example: most of us think that the civil rights movement in the U.S. represented a positive and necessary social reform of a deeply unjust and iniquitous set of social practices. But these reforms were brought about from above largely by judicial fiat, not through anything resembling a democratic process. One wonders whether if we had left the decision to democratic majorities in the American South, the civil rights agenda would have gotten very far. After all, we are talking about communities that in many cases decided (democratically) to abolish their public school systems *rather than* comply with the Court's decision in *Brown v. Board*. In such a case, most of us would on reflection probably prefer top-down decisionmaking to democratic majoritarianism, particularly of the 'populist' sort.[17]

I do not deny that in situations where a majority oppresses a minority, local democracy is not always sufficient to sort out the problems. Some help from above may be needed. The same is even truer, of course, where a minority oppresses a majority, in the manner that the white minority in South Africa oppressed the rest of society during apartheid. Here international sanctions were most helpful, but in both cases democracy among the ruling elite helped the situation of the oppressed. Although some people among the ruling elites sided with the oppressed, local democracy was not sufficient, some help was also needed from 'above'. I have no problem in acknowledging this. After all, the very point of having global democracy is to see to it that this kind of help from above, when needed, is available.

But what if democracy itself is the problem: I have also come across the objection that there is something wrong with the assumption that democracies select and pursue the right policies. This is how the objection has been stated:

> Often … [democracies] select wrong and stupid policies, as the history of Western democracy sadly attests. This is one reason why the citizens of supposedly enlightened Western democracies have consistently failed to elect leaders disposed to take the problem of global warming seriously. Similar examples, from other areas of social policy, are legion.[18]

This doesn't, however, strike me as very convincing. Of course, even democracies go wrong in politics, but I think it is rare that we can attribute their mistakes to the fact that the wrong decisions were reached in a democratic manner. Take global warming, for example. The problem here is not that it has not been possible to elect leaders who take global warming seriously. The reason that the leaders do not tend properly to the problem should rather be explained – as was the case in Chapter 4 – with reference to the tragedy of the commons nature of the problem. It is not in the interest of the citizens of an isolated nation that *their* leaders take drastic action. In other cases, the explanation why the leaders go wrong is, as was stressed by Professor Rummel, *lack* of democracy, such as, I would say, with the recent US-led war against Iraq. If the people of the United States were better informed, if they had a political system where they were effectively confronted with different ideological outlooks from competing parties, if the media system was different and more varied, I doubt that the kind of foreign policy we are now witnessing would be possible.

Of course, there is no denying that in principle enlightened despotism is superior to democracy. Even in cases where Condorcet's Jury theorem is applicable, the majority goes wrong now and then.

It is a defining characteristic of the enlightened despot that they *never* go wrong. However, we know that in practice we never find any enlightened despots, and when the despots we find go wrong, then the consequences tend to be disastrous.

The objections suggest yet something more, however: that, when some help from above is needed, the help from above should come from a system of judicial review rather than from a higher level in a democratic system. Power should be vested in a global high court of law to review laws or official acts of the world government for constitutionality or for the violation of basic principles of justice.

I disagree. My basic instinct here is to side with Alexander Bickel, who wrote *The Least Dangerous Branch*:

> The root difficulty is that judicial review is a counter-majoritarian force in our system ... when the Supreme Court declares unconstitutional a legislative act or the action of an elected executive, it thwarts the will of representatives of the actual people of the here and now; it exercises control, not on behalf of the prevailing majority, but against it. That, without mystic overtones, is what actually happens.[19]

The case for a system with judicial review is not very strong, I submit.[20] Judicial activism can go either way, to help those who are disadvantaged, or to worsen their situation. There is little evidence to the effect that, overall, their plight is improved by such a system. As Thomas Jefferson pointed out in a letter to William C. Jarvis in 1780, judges are in no way more enlightened than the rest of us:

> To consider the judges as the ultimate arbiters of all constitutional questions [is] a very dangerous doctrine indeed, and one which would place us under the despotism of an oligarchy. Our judges are as honest as other men and not more so. They have with others the same passions for party, for power, and the privilege of their corps ... and their power the more dangerous as they are in office for life and not responsible, as the other functionaries are, to the elective control. The Constitution has

erected no such single tribunal, knowing that to whatever hands confided, with the corruptions of time and party, its members would become despots. It has more wisely made all departments co-equal and co-sovereign within themselves.[21]

I do not deny, of course, that there are examples where a systematic judicial activist approach has been helpful to those who are oppressed. In particular, this kind of help may have been necessary in the United States, where there is little guarantee that the decisions of the central democratic institutions, elected in a manner conforming very well to Schumpeter's ideal of democracy, really reflect the will of the majority. In such a system judicial activism may sometimes work in accordance with, not against, the will of the (often silent) majority. One very good American example of this is indeed *Brown v. Board*. However, the *net* effects of a system of judicial review are not clearly to the advantage of people who are disadvantaged in society.

Given that no system of judicial review has *proved* to be superior to populism, there is little reason to try to implement it on a global scale. We should opt for a populist version of global democracy, I suggest. Yet, this need not be the final word about judicial review. For even if it is not part of the ideal of democracy here defended, it may be helpful in the transition from the situation in the real world today towards the ideal. In particular, it may play a transient role when the United Nations are reformed, in a manner to be described in the next chapter.

Moreover, those who side with Kant, Kelsen and Rawls and fear that a world government may become tyrannical, may find some consolation if a system of judicial review is in place. So perhaps, at the end of the day, there is room here for an ideological compromise. But is there *any* road that might lead in the direction of *any* kind of global democracy, one may wonder. There is one such road indeed, and in the next chapter I will explain how we can start walking it.

6
A road map to global democracy

1. Introduction

Is world government a realistic political goal? I have argued that, unless the goal takes the shape of a radical populist global democracy, it is not realistic. But is it realistic in the first place?

There are several traits in recent political, economical and cultural development that renders the project more realistic than ever before. I refer here to what is often termed 'globalisation'. Indeed, in particular, I think there exists a tendency towards cosmopolitanism in today's world. If we are interested in establishing a global democracy, we should take as our starting point the ideal of cosmopolitanism and the tendency towards the realisation of it. Furthermore, what many people who feel and act like true cosmopolitans tend to see as an obstacle to global democracy, the existence of one unique and mighty superpower, the United States, is nothing of the sort. The existence of one unique superpower in the world is what is needed, rather than an obstacle to global democracy, in order to render global democracy a realistic political project.

In this chapter I will show how such a project can be devised and how it should best cater for the existence of one unique superpower.

2. Cosmopolitanism

There is no unanimity about how we are to understand cosmopolitanism. On my account, a cosmopolitan is a citizen of the world. Cosmopolitanism, then, is an ideal of an all-encompassing polity, that is, an ideal of global citizenship. However, a different understanding has been standard in recent discussions. Cosmopolitanism has also been conceived of as a moral outlook (with roots in Antiquity), rather than an institutional arrangement. This is how Brian Barry uses the term:

> A cosmopolitan is, by definition, a citizen of the world. But this should not be misunderstood. Cosmopolitanism is a moral outlook, not an institutional prescription. The first people to call themselves cosmopolitans were the Stoics, who already belonged to a state that encompassed the whole of the civilized world ... The point for them was to indicate that they were, in the first instance, human beings living in a world of human beings and only incidentally members of polities. It is this spirit that animates contemporary cosmopolitanism, which is a moral stance consisting of three elements: individualism, equality, and universality.[1]

Even if Barry would count this as 'misunderstanding', this is not the way I use the word 'cosmopolitan'. On my use of the word in the present context it *is* an institutional prescription (to the effect that a global citizenship should exist) and an institutional prescription first and foremost. This means that cosmopolitanism, a global citizenship, as here conceived, is in principle consistent with all kinds of rule: democratic; autocratic; plutocratic; dictatorial; and so forth. Yet, I would agree that, if a rationale behind cosmopolitanism exists, it should acknowledge some kind of individualism, equality and universality.

But does such a rationale exist? Is cosmopolitanism as such a viable ideal?

93

3. Is cosmopolitanism a viable ideal?

Even on a rather legalistic understanding of the notion of global citizenship it is clear that, to some extent, such a global citizenship does exist already. Not only are the actions that are open to national governments severely restricted by the existence of powerful economic actors in the global arena, but their sovereignty with respect to their own citizens withers. There are international conventions, such as the United Nations Charter on Human Rights, which are binding on all citizens in the world, irrespective of nationality. The same is true of documents such as the Charters of the Nuremberg and Tokyo War Crimes Tribunals, the Helsinki Declaration, the Covenant on Civil and Political Rights and the European Convention on Human Rights. There are also institutions such as the International Court of Justice in The Hague (referred to in Chapter 2 in relation to the United States' attempt to overthrow the Sandinistas government in Nicaragua), capable of punishing (some) actions at variance with them.

Moreover, recent proceedings at the International Criminal Court, a permanent judicial body to prosecute war crimes, genocide and crimes against humanity, hold out hope for the future, despite the United States' refusal to recognise its jurisdiction and participate in its proceedings. The court is able to investigate and prosecute those individuals accused of crimes against humanity, genocide and war crimes if national courts are unwilling or unable to investigate or prosecute such crimes. The International Criminal Court will also help to defend the rights of those, such as women and children, who have often had little recourse to justice.

On a less legalistic understanding of the notion of a global citizenship, it is clear that there are all sorts of political decisions taken in the world that are *de facto* binding for all citizens in the world; I think here of decisions taken by international organisations such as the WTO, the IMF, the World Bank and various transnational judicial forums. Furthermore, and even more importantly, there are decisions taken by individual governments, the United States government in particular, which, as a matter of fact, are binding for all citizens of the globe: I refer here to decisions to prohibit the growing of certain crops (such as coca in South America), which are *de facto* binding on all world citizens; of all kinds of so-called anti-terrorist measures, which are carried out on a global scale.

In a global world, moreover, and this is a point of growing importance, where people travel and where trade is global, it is also clear that, even a law adopted by a national parliament is, in fact, binding all citizens of the world. If the South African parliament, for example, decides to tax certain products, these taxes will have to be paid by anyone who travels to, or establishes commerce with, South Africa.

It must suffice here to note that it would be vain to attempt to argue that no ideal of a cosmopolitan citizenship could be realised. We may safely argue from what exists, or, at least, from what is slowly coming into existence, to what is possible. The problem to be faced is to determine if there is a way of 'democratising' global citizenship rather than accepting that democracy withers. Is there of way of exchanging a flourishing global democracy for many withering national democracies?

This is how we should go about it, if we want to explore this possibility.

4. Representative democracy on a global level

We saw in the previous chapter that the only realistic notion of global democracy is cast in radical populist terms. What is needed is nothing less than a world parliament, elected in a representative manner, ensuring that the laws that are adopted by it are, in a manner of speaking, the laws that would have been enacted had it been possible for the global population to meet under the oaks, to discuss various different proposals carefully and, finally, to reach their decision through the application of majority rule.

Is there a way of approaching such a situation? Is there any way a trustworthy road map towards global democracy can be drawn? The following idea of a cosmopolitan citizenship and a world government could be adumbrated. We build here on the only available existing institution, the UN. In the interests of cosmopolitan citizenship together with a world government the UN would be reformed in the following manner (I rely here on ideas previously put forward in my *Populist Democracy. A Defence* (1992) – similar proposals, some of them less and others more specific have been made by many other thinkers who have addressed the issue).[2]

The general assembly would be divided into two houses. At least to start with, the existing one remains as a kind of House of Lords. The second one, having the function of a House of Commons, which from now on we can call a Global Peoples' Assembly, is elected in a proportionate manner by the world population and the representatives that take their place in the Peoples' Assembly will have one vote each. The elections must be supervised and accepted by representatives of the UN. All countries are allowed to take part in the elections.

If there are countries where the government hesitates to allow free elections, then the seats from these regions of the world will remain empty. This will provide a strong incentive for the governments to overcome their fears of free elections. Consider, for example, the prospect that India will elect their representatives, while China will leave their seats vacant. How would this be viewed by the Chinese public at large!

If all the most important countries agree to take part in the elections, a very interesting view of the world will emerge when we see the representatives assemble: a third of all the representatives will be from China and India! Or, is this perhaps a problem? Some advocates of world government have thought so. A. C. Ewing, for example, wants to restrict the representation from the most densely populated regions of the world:

> Without casting any reflections whatever on the Indians or Chinese, it must be admitted that few Englishmen or Americans would care to be governed by a body in which these two countries had together four or five times as much say as the Anglo-Saxon peoples.[3]

This qualification is unreasonable, and it is certainly unacceptable to the Indians and the Chinese. So I think rather that the fact described here is something that should teach many (of us) Western people a lesson. If we compromise the populist democratic ideal from the start, the political struggle in defence of it will be lost.

There is another problem, which is real, but of little consequence, that is, some nation-states are too small to be entitled to any representative in the world parliament. If the parliament consists of, say, one thousand representatives, who are representative of a global population consisting of six billion people, it takes a population consisting of some six million people in order to have the right to a representative. There are two main ways of approaching this practical problem. One is to compromise the ideal and grant representatives also to these small countries at the cost of large countries. A better way, it seems to me, is to construct special constituencies, not following national borders, in order to allow the citizens of small states to cast their votes in the elections. After all, those who are elected are not supposed to represent their nations, but rather political parties having a stand on problems to do with peace, global justice and the environment.

As a matter of fact, this means that it might be a good idea eventually to get rid of the reliance on nation-states when constituencies are constructed. Why not accept, for example, that the European Union is one constituency rather than many. In that way different parties can compete within the EU for the support of its citizens, and representatives from more than one party can be elected from this region.

The House of Lords of the UN would consist of representatives of national governments according to the system, one country, one vote.

Once a world parliament has been established there should also be world government. How should it be elected? I suppose that the two houses of the General Assembly together could select some representatives to it. But it is also natural to accept that there will be some permanent members of it, such as, for example, representatives from the governments of China, India, Russia, the EU and the United

States. Unless these powers feel that they can keep control over world politics, global citizenship will not exist in the first place.

History has witnessed many failed attempts to reform the UN. Most efforts to reform the structure and intended to increase its effectiveness have been met with a veto from the United States. Would the same happen to this proposal? I think not, at least if two important provisos are satisfied. First, the initiative behind the reform must come from the world population as a whole, not from governments exclusively. Secondly, the reform must start in the right way, that is, with the introduction of a democratically elected Peoples' Assembly.

How could the United States government, be it Republican or Democrat, defend its repudiation of *such* a reform? After all, the United States has many times fought wars in the name of democracy! Moreover, the United States administration has often claimed that the UN, in its existing form, is too much in the hands of non-democratic governments. American politicians would have a hard time explaining to their voters why they opposed such a democratic form of the UN.

If the General Assembly (the Peoples' Assembly) lacks power, if the main powers in the world in general, and the United States in particular, feel that the system is safe, then I see no reason why such a constitutional reform of the UN would not be possible. I am inclined to defend this 'ecumenical' stance. However, it might be thought to be squeamish not to abolish the privileged position of some of the main powers in the UN immediately. Johan Galtung, for one, thinks so, and advocates a more sectarian position:

> To the argument that this is the condition for Big Powers being in the UN, a perfectly reasonable answer would be that if having special privileges is the condition for their membership then they do not belong in the key organization of a world heading for global democracy.[4]

I do not deny that the answer suggested by Galtung may be 'reasonable', but I doubt that it is wise. For strategic reasons it is extremely important to get the Peoples' Assembly in place. Once it exists we may rely in our democratic enterprise to a large extent on its appetite for power. Of course, the goal in the long run is that the House of Lords should be abolished (or, perhaps, it too should be elected by the citizens of the world and stay in place?) and, more importantly, that the Peoples' Assembly be sovereign. However, this being said, I must also confess that I think there is something to Galtung's point, so I do not definitely want to set it to one side. As a matter of fact, I will return to it in the next chapter, where I return also to the idea discussed in the previous chapter that, as a kind of ideological compromise, it might be a good idea to establish a global high court capable of striking down laws enacted by the Peoples' Assembly of the world parliament. The existence of such a high court, capable of judicial review, may render easier the abolishment of the privileged position of the big powers.

5. The military question

One of the most urgent tasks for the world government to deal with, as we saw in Chapter 2, is to see to it that international law and order is established. To the extent that democracies do not wage war against one another, and to the extent that the establishment of the directly elected world parliament leads to democracy all over the world, this task may not be very demanding. However, we have found reasons to doubt that democracy as such is an obstacle to war and some states may stay out of the global democratic system for some time, so the objective of keeping global peace may, indeed, be quite real. This takes military force. As Hobbes put the point, 'covenants, without the sword, are but words, and of no strength to secure a man at all'.[5] How could a global military force be established?

I suggest the following solution, in line with the original intentions of the UN Charter. Those countries who feel that they already have a rather secure situation should be encouraged immediately to give up their military defence in exchange for guaranteed borders (by the world government). They should also be required to keep some military resources available for peace-keeping missions ventured upon by the world government, and the world government only.

Since military resources are cost consuming, there will exist a drive to adopt this policy. To adopt it would mean economic gain coupled with high international standing. Yet, for all that, is it at all realistic to hope that such a process will ever get going? History presents us with few examples of this but then, the situation in the world today with one dominating superpower is different from that which we have experienced for a very long time. It is crucial, of course, that some countries break the ground; then it would not be far-fetched to believe that many will follow suit. Crucial to success here is that on consideration people in general find the idea attractive.

I have tried to find out what the Swedes think about my proposal. When writing a book on the ethics of killing (in Swedish) I had a survey carried out: eighty-eight per cent of Swedes were in favour of a military defence (ninety per cent of the men, eighty-six per cent of the women). I then asked the following question: If Sweden could give up its military defence in exchange for security guarantees from the United Nations, while contributing to the world organisation some military peace-keeping forces, do you think Sweden should do so? Here thirty-six per cent (forty-two per cent of the men and thirty-one per cent of the women) said 'yes' while fifity-seven per cent said 'no').

I found this result encouraging. If more than a third of the population supports the proposal, even before it has been subject to public debate, it should not be impossible for a dedicated cosmopolitan political movement to gain a majority! So I repeated my study in two more countries: Norway and Germany. The result from Norway was not very encouraging; very few sympathised with the proposal. However, the result from Germany was stunning. Here a slight *majority* prefered giving up the military force to the UN in exchange for the kind of guarantees I have here described. Even more impressive are the results of a global survey, conducted by the Chicago Council on Global Affairs together with WorldPublicOpinion.org. Here it surfaces, according to the press release, that:

Publics around the world favor dramatic steps to strengthen the United Nations, including giving it the power to have its own standing peacekeeping force, to regulate the international arms trade and to investigate human rights abuses. Large majorities believe the United Nations Security Council should have the right to authorize military force to prevent nuclear proliferation, genocide and terrorism. However support is not as robust among the publics polled for accepting UN decisions that go against their countries' preferences. The poll results were released on May 10, 2007.[6]

In a situation where there exists only one superpower, it is plausible, therefore, to think that the entire world will follow suit rather swiftly (perhaps with the exception of some 'rogue' states, 'contained' by the UN peace-keeping forces, and perhaps also for Norway with its stubborn nationalist sentiments); the sole exception to this, I suspect, would be the single military superpower: the United States.

At last a situation is reached, foreshadowed by A. C. Ewing (1947), where the difficulty would be 'not to persuade states to limit their armaments, but to persuade them to contribute their rightful share in armaments to the security of the whole'.[7] Or, as Bentham put a similar point 150 years earlier:

On the contrary, whatsoever nation should act the start of the other in making the proposal to reduce and fix the amount of its armed force, would crown itself with everlasting honour. The risk would be nothing – the gain certain. This gain would be, the giving an incontrovertible demonstration of its own disposition to peace, and of the opposite disposition in the other nation in case of its rejecting the proposal.

There is one caveat that needs to be addressed, however. Even if it is not difficult to find examples of possible early birds, such as Sweden and Germany, there may exist some refractory states besides the United States. In particular, it has been claimed, that China and India may not be eager to abolish their military defences and to join a democratised UN. Instead the Chinese and Indian leaderships may speculate that in the future China or India will be able to succeed the United States as the dominant world power. This is one way in which Donald Weadon, an international lawyer, has made this point with respect to China:

> What is the best metaphor for this situation, which lacks both the linearity of checkers and the exquisite dynamism of chess? Perhaps it is the national game of China – *wei ch'i* or 'Go' – where control of the board is the crucial objective and the timeline is slow and deliberate. As in this 4,000-year-old board game, China is using economic wedge manoeuvres to expand its financial influence, harden its economic achievements into political interests, and ultimately achieve control of the 'board'.[8]

Similar views have been put forward with respect to India. However, I doubt that this is a wise strategy for India or China to adopt. It will take a very long time to catch up with the United States, even in mere economic terms, and it is not certain that it will ever happen. As we know from the discussion about global injustices in Chapter 3, we often forget that the differences in absolute terms may widen even when, relatively speaking, they are shrinking. This is a speculation put forward by the economist Peter Svedberg about India:

> First an optimistic scenario: we postulate that India's per capita income growth will be a steady 6 per cent in the years to come (about 2 percentage points higher than during the 1990s), while it remains at 2 per cent in the US. In 20 years time, the per capita income in India will reach P$7,180, and increase in *relative* terms to 15.5 per cent of that in the US ... The *absolute* gap, however, will widen to about P$39,180. The outcome is a *convergence* of relative per capita incomes, but a *divergence* of absolute incomes. In this scenario, the per capita income in India in the middle of the present century (P$41,260) will, by far, have surpassed the 2000 income in the US (P$31,200). Furthermore,

the ratio of per capita incomes has increased to 49 per cent. Yet, the absolute gap in per capita income has grown to P$42,740. In this example, a decrease in the absolute gap will not appear until around 2050. It will hence take half a century – or close to two generations – before the absolute difference in per capita income *begins to close*, even if India's income were to grow three times faster than that of the US. In a less optimistic scenario, where the postulated future annual per capita income growth in India is more moderate (3 per cent), but still higher than in the US (2 per cent), the absolute income gap will continue to grow far into the 22nd century.[9]

And Nobel Prize Laureate Gary Becker strikes a similar cautious note about China:

China's economic growth since it freed agriculture from the oppressive hand of government has been spectacular, averaging some 7–10 per cent per year in real GDP since 1980, even allowing for some inflation in the official numbers. It is becoming a leading destination of foreign investment, one of the world's biggest exporters, and among the largest users of oil and other natural resources.

Its potential seems to be so limitless, after awakening from a slumber that lasted for centuries, that many are already forecasting that China will replace the United States during the 21st century as the leading economic power. Perhaps these forecasts will be correct – my crystal ball is very cloudy – but some cautionary comments are needed because we have heard that tune before[10]

And he goes on to comparisons with Japan, Germany, the Soviet Union and other cases only to conclude:

I am not saying that China will not become the leading economic nation, but rather that it is far too early to tell. The many failed predictions about Japan and other nations should make us modest about such long-term predictions. Perhaps India will become the leader – it has strengths (and weaknesses) that China lacks – or maybe Brazil if it can finally get its act together.[11]

The gap between American spending on military resources and the spending of other countries is also formidable. For example, in 2006 the United States spent US$ 528.7 billion while China's military expenditure was US$ 49.5 billion (in US$ – 2005).[12]

A wise Chinese or Indian leadership would rather argue, therefore, in the following terms. If the UN can provide safeguards with respect to existing borders, then it is a very good idea to give up the arms race with the United States. After all, it seems to be part of received wisdom that it was the arms race with the United States that brought down the Soviet Union. By giving up the arms race, China and India gain a competitive advantage over the United States in the competition for economic power. Of course, it may even be dangerous for just one of these countries, China or India, to challenge the United States, while the other takes advantage of not taking part in the arms race. Furthermore, China and India are the countries that stand to gain most from global democracy in the sense that, when they have some vital national interests at stake in the world parliament, they would have an enormous say. Remember that the Chinese and Indian peoples will each control one-sixth of the seats in the Peoples' Assembly in the world parliament. This is a very good reason for them to join the movement for global democracy.

This is, of course, a corresponding reason for relatively small countries that have been used in the past to ruling the world, such as the United States, the United Kingdom, France, Russia and Japan to be sceptical with respect to global democracy. Yet, at the end of the day, it will be difficult for them to stay out of the process, at least if there is strong worldwide popular support for it.

However, is there any hope that the United States will ever follow suit? Only a few years ago the United States adopted as official policy that no power should be allowed to develop any military strength that parallels that of the United States. According to a thirty-three-page White House document, published on 20 September 2002 and submitted to Congress, no state will be allowed to challenge the military supremacy of the United States. A key pillar of American national security policy would be to 'dissuade future military competition', the document states. The essential role of American military strength is to 'build and maintain our defenses beyond challenge … Our forces will be strong enough to dissuade potential adversaries from pursuing a military build-up in hopes of surpassing, or equalling, the power of the United States'.

There is no need to complain about this arrogant move by the United States administration – the appropriate reaction is to turn the other cheek. The rest of the world ought to challenge the United States' military arrogance with radical pacifism and successive, systematic global disarmament, or so I have argued. The rest of the world should do so in the hope that this would make an impression on the Americans at large. Is this overly optimistic?

It is not. When the rest of the world has disarmed there will be much discontent in the United States that one nation should bear this kind of cost exclusively. This may seem especially strange if no rival military powers exist in the world. So there will be a strong incentive in the United States to disarm and to join the rest of the world. Why should the United States *compete* with the UN in an endeavour to make the world safe for freedom and democracy, is a question people in the United States could come ask. Or, is the United States exploiting the rest of the world economically to such extent that, if it cannot sustain the system through military means, there will be a net cost to the *average* American citizen?

I am certainly no expert on international economic relations, but I very much doubt that imperialist exploitative relations that are of course in place play such a significant role, and unless they do, I suggest that it seems rather plausible that there will be popular dissent over American military costs. It might be objected, of course, that what matters is not whether the average American would stand to gain or lose, once the military costs were abolished, but what the average American would *believe* about this. Could not the military expenditure be retained through the production of the right kind of ideology? This is certainly a possibility, but this only means that it is an important political task incumbent on all those who adhere to the global democratic ideal to expose and dismantle this kind of ideology. It is certainly a *sine qua non* to such an exposure that there be no *competing* military forces left in the world.

As a matter of fact, this is the main reason for being an EU sceptic, while being enthusiastic with respect to cosmopolitanism. I used to argue differently (in my *Populist Democracy*), when, like most people who have written about a world government, I conceived of the road to the establishment of it as a series of steps, where regions first unite, and then form the global form of unity. I see now, in a new historic situation, that this is mistaken. These regions would rather compete with each other than unite. Also the idea that Europe has a special mission in history, recently advocated by Habermas and Derrida[13] is no less arrogant than the official United States policy described above. It is, indeed, the emergence of one absolute superpower that prepares the way to a world government.

6. Multinationals and global democracy

I have argued that there is a way to overcome resistance based in nation-states to the idea of global democracy. However, I have also met the objection that there may be another kind of obstacle, which might prove even more refractory, and it has to do with multinational companies. One of the reasons that we need global democracy has to do with the existence of such companies, of course. In the existing world order, if a government restricts or regulates an industry, for environmental reasons, for example, the company can choose to move its production abroad rather than comply with the regulations. So, in many ways, the multinational companies find means of bullying and punishing the governments of poor nations. As the point has been put forward by David Beetham:

> This freedom of movement by multinationals tends to penalize governments which seek to maintain standards of social welfare, environmental regulation or tax regimes ... many of the measures which governments have used in the past to

develop a coherent industrial policy for their country are no longer possible.[14]

All this means that we need a world government to put forward regulations with respect to multinational companies. However, if multinationals feel that they may be more strictly regulated in their dealings in a global democracy than they are in today's anarchistic world order, then this may mean that their protest to the establishment of global democracy may be very strong. Perhaps powerful multinational companies will even be able to obstruct the road to global democracy, then. And perhaps their obstruction, considering their economic power, will be decisive.

How we should assess the strength of this objection to the feasibility of global democracy has much to do with what we (and the executives and owners of the multinational companies) can reasonably expect from a global democracy in terms of radical attacks against the liberty of the multinational companies. Of course, if the establishment of global democracy means world socialist revolution, in the style of Lenin and Trotsky, then the multinational companies will organise a very strong resistance indeed. However, there is little that indicates that the establishment of global democracy would mean a global transition socialism. The natural parallel is rather with the establishment of various national kinds of democracy. In some places, where the transition to democracy has been coupled with strong social ambitions, such as in Spain in the 1930s and in Chile in the 1970s the opposition has been violent, of course. But the introduction of democracy in many other countries, where it has not been coupled with strong social ambitions, has been peaceful. Even when the introduction of democracy has meant a transition to a welfare state, there has been plenty of room for big business to flourish. The Scandinavian example is here instructive. The transition to a democratic welfare state has been tolerated by those who are in control of decisive means of economic power. The reason is that they have found the transition either to their advantage, or at least as a kind of reasonable compromise, guaranteeing peaceful conditions and stable institutions in the foreseeable future. There is interesting research on this topic upon which it is possible to draw also when it comes to the transition to global democracy.[15]

It might be difficult to understand *why* multinational companies would accept an order where their freedom is in many ways curtailed. Here it is important to avoid a simple misunderstanding, however. Each multinational company has, when it decides where to invest in the existing world order, an incentive to take advantage of low wages, poor social conditions and so forth. If it does not take advantage of such, from its own restricted point of view, 'assets', then someone else will do so, and it will be relatively worse placed in the fierce competition on the market. In the circumstances, it may be economically rational to resort to costly measures such as threats and bribes in order to have one's way. An executive may be willing to take a not negligible risk of ending up in court. However, if *no* one is allowed to take advantage of assets such as these, then it means no *competitive* drawback not to do so. Moreover, a secure global order may be advantageous to commerce in general. Peace, a competent and self-confident workforce, may be come to be seen as assets rather than as costs, at least to those firms that are not closely connected to the military industrial complex.

It is reasonable to assume, then, that the opposition from the multinational capital, which will undoubtedly be there, is not invincible. There may even be some enlightened capitalists of the George Soros type around, who see global democracy as a possibility rather than a problem.

7. Conclusion

I have been very brief and sketchy in this chapter. It would be ridiculous to treat the subject otherwise. No one can make a reliable and very detailed blueprint for global democracy. I assume, however, that I have now shown that the idea of a sovereign world government is not completely utopian. I have indicated one way in which it may come about. Global democracy cannot be won in a day, however; if ever established, it will be established as the result of global political struggle. And it is up to the global political movement, dedicated to the cause, to mould a more realistic policy when the various possibilities arise and when new institutions unfold. What is needed is a situation where many people in the world follow the example of Gary Davies and join various new attempts to create a citizenship of the world. If they do, then there is no reason to think that global democracy *cannot* be established in that way.

But will such a movement ever arise? We have seen that unless we resort to global democracy we will have to live with war, global injustices and environmental problems. This fact alone is a strong reason to expect that such a movement will be formed. Moreover, it is not only a matter of establishing institutions that can deal with these problems. It is also a matter of being personally involved in the solution of them. Parents in the rich part of our globe hesitate to tell their children about the exact details of the situation of the world when it comes to problems to do with war, injustices and environmental problems, while parents in the poor parts of the world have a hard enough time trying to keep their children healthy and alive through these problems. It would be a relief for them all if they knew, not only that there were institutions in the world that were dedicated to solving problems to do with war, injustices and the environment, but if they knew also that these institutions involved them in the process as well. If they knew that they had a say, if they could find it meaningful to voice opinions about how best to settle the problems, then they would not hesitate to inform their children about the situation of the world.

All this is promised by the idea of global democracy put forward here. So, if it is realistic, if it can come about through hard political struggle, is it not self-evident that such political struggle will soon see the day? I submit that it is, but before I feel I can convince my readers of this, there is one problem that must first be settled. Some thinkers seem to be prepared to argue that global democracy, far from being a political goal worthy of our aspirations, would be a real dystopia. If these thinkers are right, then the prospects for global democracy are indeed bleak.

These people are wrong, however, and I will try to show this in the next chapter where I formulate, address and rebut various arguments to the effect that global democracy is a dystopia. Important thinkers such as Immanuel Kant, Hans Kelsen and John Rawls to the contrary notwithstanding, global democracy *is* desirable in its own right. So the time is now ripe for the formation of the necessary political movement to put it in place.

7
Is global democracy desirable?

1. Introduction

We have seen that unless global democracy is established we will have to bear the problems of perpetual war, global injustice and the degradation of the environment. We have also seen that the idea of global democracy is not altogether utopian. But is it desirable as such? Should we perhaps just tolerate perpetual war, global injustice and severe environmental problems, rather than resorting to global democracy? Are there problems inherent in the notion of a single global democracy that are so severe that it would be better to abstain from following the road map that was drawn in the previous chapter? Should we even refrain from the first, seemingly innocuous step towards global democracy described in the previous chapter: the introduction of a directly elected Peoples' Assembly of the United Nations in case this might put us on the slippery slope towards a world government?

Some people seem to think so, and they have put forward some very strong arguments in defence of their position. In this chapter I will discuss and rebut these arguments. These arguments are mainly those stemming from a lack of democracy (a global democracy would be a sham), communitarianism (there is a lack of community in the world at large, and such a community is a prerequisite for a common democracy), lack of economic integration (and such

111

integration is a prerequisite for a common democracy), and, finally, the fear that global democracy may come to mean global tyranny. I will discuss them in order below.

2. *Lack of democracy*

One objection to the adumbrated reform would undoubtedly be that it is lacking in democratic quality and, if we apply it to the *early* stages of the road map here designed, this objection is certainly correct. The decisions taken by the three bodies (the two houses of the general assembly and the world government) could very well be 'democratic' in the sense that each decision reflects the will of the body which takes it. It is desirable that a democratic procedure is adhered to here. Moreover, if the Peoples' Assembly is elected in a strictly proportionate manner, it may make sense to say of its decisions that they reflect the will of the people of the world. This being a fact will be a strong impetus to popular political participation on a global scale and, hence, to an urge for further democratisation. However, as has been stressed, the decisions taken by the Peoples' Assembly of the General Assembly will be of minor importance. So even if the Peoples' Assembly of the General Assembly could be representative of the world population, in a straightforward sense (once elections have been arranged on a global level), by their decisions they would not be able to make much difference to world politics. It has also been stressed that there would have to be a right to a veto from the Security Council against any bills taken by the General Assembly – at least in the near future. Furthermore, there would have to be a right to a veto from representatives of the permanent members of the Security Council (the World Government) against almost any kind of political action upon which a majority of the members want to embark. All this means that the objection that a political system such as the one outlined would not mean that the will of the world population would in any way be decisive to the political decisions reached by the World Government, would certainly be correct.

Is this a relevant objection to this kind of institution? I am somewhat ambivalent on this point. My main inclination, however, is to argue in the following manner: the objection is true but irrelevant. After all, if these institutions were established, and I refer in particular to the Peoples' Assembly, then there would exist an important instrument for future democratisation. In the same manner that the European Parliament is eager to obtain more power and influence, it is reasonable to assume that the Peoples' Assembly of the UN would be eager to obtain power. Also, in the same manner that the European Parliament has an important role to play when public political discussions take place that mould the general public opinion within the EU, the Peoples' Assembly of the UN would mould world opinion.

However, there is an important difference between the EU and the world. While within the EU there are many strong nations competing for influence, world politics bears little semblance to this and this leads to a serious follow up on the objection from democracy. A World Government elected along the aforementioned lines would not only be largely unresponsive to the political opinion held by the world population, it would, in fact, be in the grips of the United States administration. The system adumbrated would mean that the United States would rule the world through the UN, or, as in relation to the second Iraq war (in 2003), when they fail to obtain support from the UN for their military adventures, they will carry on with such adventures *irrespective* of what the UN decides.

Again, following my basic intuition, we must conclude that this follow up on the objection from democracy is true but irrelevant: the United States rules the world anyway! We should instead think here, not of the present, but of the future. We should compare how the process towards national democracy in many countries has taken place. It is the rule, not the exception, that institutions have been established that, at first, have had no effective say in politics, however, eventually, they have become decisive. The establishment of a political order need not be the solution to any immediate problem to be of value. Even a national parliament, lacking completely in power, may be (has often been) the beginning of a process that has led to a democratic order. This is how we ought to conceive of the establishment of a world parliament and world government. Once the institutions are in place it will be a feasible goal to aspire to more democracy. There will be an urge to get rid of the right to any veto, to get rid of the permanent national representation and so forth. The final goal would be to establish a sovereign world parliament, which elects a responsible world government.

There is a possible egalitarian or left-wing follow up on this objection, however. When I discussed my road map to global democracy I also discussed possible opposition to global democracy from economic elites who are today capable of competing with one another by bribing, threatening and bullying national governments in order to have their way. I argued that such resistance might be possible to overcome if restrictions against such behaviour on the part of big business are impartially handled; then the existence of these restrictions would mean that there would be no *relative* disadvantage to any one firm in particular. I also argued, which is more important in the present context, that a transition to global democracy may be feasible if it doesn't take too radical a redistributive form. This is the lesson we must draw from the introduction of democracy on a national level,[1] and global democracy is hardly any different in this respect. Now, it is reasonable to believe that global democracy will not be radically redistributive, but this, of course, means that it would lack some of the attractions that egalitarians have seen in democracy.

Here the proper attitude, it seems to me, is to hope for improvement in the very long term, when global democracy is safely in place. Then the time may also be ripe also for some more advanced social global reforms. Here we can only speculate, however, so there is no denying that there is something to the objection that global democracy is likely to deliver less than many egalitarians would hope for.

Now, even if what I have just described may be conceived of as not radical enough when viewed from the point of view of an egalitarian ideology, it may be conceived of as too radical when viewed from a purely institutional point of view. Some may want to find a middle path when it comes to institutional design. A way of finding a middle path could be to introduce a system of legal review. Instead of just dropping, when the time is right, the United States veto, a global high court could be introduced at an early stage of the process: a high court with the right to strike down laws enacted by the global Peoples' Assembly. Since this system holds such a sway over many American thinkers, lawyers and politicians, it may also turn out to be attractive to the United States government. It may, therefore, be a way of facilitating the step from a situation where the United States (and other influential nations) have a right to veto decisions taken by the world government, to a situation where this right has been abolished once and for all.

However, I have confessed to a certain ambivalence on this point. The reasoning put forward here, to the effect that the argument arising from democracy should be set aside as true but irrelevant, may be fine as far as it goes, but what if people at large are not prepared to dedicate themselves to global democracy unless they feel that some kind of direct results can be foreseen? They may feel that the ecumenical and reformist view here advocated does not really give them what they want. They may feel also, not only that it is unfair to introduce a high court only to seduce the Americans to join the global democracy, but also that, once in place, the court may come to stay there and hence curtail democracy – as they conceive of it – indefinitely. We should here also bear in mind Johan Galtung's sectarian claim, quoted in the previous chapter, to the effect that if some nations (the United States in particular) are not prepared to take part in a democratised version of the UN unless they have the right to veto decisions they dislike, then we had better go along with our global democratic project without them. We should do so in the hope that, when global democratic institutions are firmly established, the United States and other refractory nations will eventually follow suit and become members on equal terms. It is easy to feel a strong attraction to this strategy but is it likely that it will succeed? Is this a feasible strategy in the attempt to establish global democracy?

As I have indicated, even if I am inclined to reject this strategy, I am not prepared definitely to read it out of court. So perhaps a good idea is not to have any strong stance with respect to the question, or to the question of whether there should be a global system of judicial review. It will probably not be decided by any rational argument put forward in a cool hour but rather in the heat of future global political action; so perhaps we should allow the future political movement in defence of global democracy to settle the matter when time has come to do so. In any case, there seems to be an answer to the argument arising from a lack of democracy. Either it can be tackled in the very long term through an ecumenical and reformist strategy to which I feel inclined, or it can be dealt with more swiftly by adoption of Galtung's more sectarian and radical approach.

3. Communitarianism

There exits an argument stemming from communitarianism to the effect that global citizenship is not desirable. The point of departure of this argument is the idea that citizenship should go together with a kind of communality. Citizenship, in this view, presupposes immersion in a common language, a common culture, a set of values, a common history and so forth. It is not difficult, but not very meaningful in the present context, to find radical statements of this position from thinkers such as Alasdair MacIntyre, Michael Sandel, Charles Taylor and Michael Walzer.[2] It is noteworthy, however, that even such a moderate thinker as the Canadian communitarian philosopher Will Kymlicka comes close to stating it when, for example, he writes:

> Democracy requires us to trust, and to make sacrifices for, those who do not share our interests and goals. The emergence of issue-specific transnational identities may explain why Greenpeace members are willing to make sacrifices for the environment around the world but it doesn't explain why Greenpeace members are willing to make sacrifices for, say, ethnocultural minorities around the world, particularly those who may demand the right to engage in practices harmful to the environment. Democracy requires the adjudication of conflicting interests, and so works best when there is some sort of common identity that transcends these conflicting interests. Within

Is global democracy desirable?

nation-states, a common national identity ideally transcends differences between pro-development and pro-environment groups, and enables some level of trust and solidarity between them. It is difficult to see what services this function at the transnational level.[3]

To my mind, even in this less radical form, I find this idea wrong. The premise upon which it is based, the notion that a common citizenship requires the kind of communality here put forward, is false. It is false if taken as an empirical statement and it is equally false if taken as a statement of an ideal. It is neither necessary nor desirable that people who belong to the same political unit share language, culture, basic values, or anything of the kind. All these things are important to our well-being and our sense of identity, but it is equally important that they are allowed to flourish in small and voluntary associations, not within political units. This is to do with the fact that political units are not, or, when they are, are only to some extent, voluntary. We are not only born into political units (as we are born into cultures), but it may prove very difficult and even impossible for us to leave them. But then they should not take a form, which could mean that we would feel suffocated once we found out that we were destined to belong to any one of them in particular. I have discussed this theme elsewhere in this general form, and will not belabour the point in the present context.[4]

Even more importantly, in the present context, when *global* democracy is discussed the argument arising from communitarianism lacks force. On a global level it would be absurd to seek close unity among all people as this is not what is needed nor is it desirable. When a global democracy is established, this is in order better to handle pressing problems to do with peace, justice and the environment. A world government should deal with these problems, but it should not meddle with all sorts of other problems, which are better left for national and local governments where they should be delegated to the appropriate levels.

It might be thought that the solution to problems of global justice requires a close unity. This would be true if the solution to these

117

problems could best be achieved through heavy taxes that redistribute resources among individual people on the globe. However, as has been argued in Chapter 3, this is not a realistic approach to global injustices. If it were, the struggle to eliminate them would indeed be in vain for exactly the reasons that some communitarians have put forward. People are not prepared to pay heavy taxes if they do not feel any solidarity with those who are at the receiving end of the system, and they are not likely to do so on a global level.[5] However, such a redistributive scheme is not required in order to establish global justice. What is required is merely a common understanding that local empowerment all over the world is a reasonable requirement, as well as a shared interest in global peace and a good environment. It is not very controversial to assume that most people in the world share *these* interests. These are not basic values but rather values that people can come to favour for all sorts of reasons, through what John Rawls has famously called an overlapping consensus.

There is a different way of understanding the communitarian argument, however. Even if a close community is not necessary to the functioning of a political system, small political units may be of interest if we want to cherish certain typical communitarian values. If a close ethnic community is part of a nation where it lives as a minority, it might feel threatened by the majority. It might be better for it to become independent in order to avoid oppression from the alien majority culture. Is this a good argument against a global political community? I think not. As a matter of fact, it seems to be a good argument in *defence* of a global political community.

There is no way to solve, with recourse to ethnic cleansing, secession and the like, all the problems in the world where minorities in nation-states feel threatened by alien majoritarian cultures. The problem is that people marry, conceive children, make friends and so forth across ethnic lines. So people in the modern world just have to accept that they live together with people from different cultures. However, if they do so in closed nation-states, where there is such a thing as a majority culture, the situation may indeed be perceived of as suffocating when viewed from the point of view of the members of the minority culture. In a global political community there is no such thing as *a* majority culture. Hence there is no need for any minority culture in particular to feel threatened by it.

As a matter of fact, even the establishment of supranational powers, such as the European Union, may render more tolerable the life of minority cultures in regions of nation-states. It may, for example, be more acceptable for a Basque nationalist to accept that he or she is a citizen of the European Union than of Spain. And the reason is that there is no such thing as a European common culture based on any very particular basic values.

This insistence that *basic* values need not be shared on the globe is not to say that *no* values need to be shared if a world government were to be installed. Here the values constitutive of 'cosmopolitanism' in Brian Barry's sense of the word come to mind: individualism; equality; and universality. Certainly, at least a common adherence to democracy of some sort (for reasons that can take a variety of forms) would be necessary. So unless national democracy is established in at least a majority of nations, and in the largest ones in particular, the idea of a world government is a non-starter.

However, the very idea of starting to democratise the UN institutions is to render possible a worldwide transformation towards democracy. A kind of 'democratic determinism' put in motion through the establishment of the Peoples' Assembly of the UN is intended to achieve this task.[6]

It might be thought that, in the aforementioned argument, I dismiss the problem of a common language too easily. Our language is a sign of our identity, and perhaps we need not share this kind of identity with our fellow citizens. However, we do need to communicate with them, at least if the political process where collective decisions are reached is to have a civilised form. But how is it possible for all the citizens on the globe to communicate when we speak so many different languages? It was Saint Augustine who raised this objection to the idea of a world government:

> For if two men, each ignorant of the other's language, meet and
> are compelled … to remain together, then it is easier for dumb

animals, even of different kinds, to associate together than for them, though both are human beings.[7]

But had not Rome succeeded in spreading its own *lingua franca*? Had it not established a world order? It had, Saint Augustine conceded, 'but at what a cost has this unity been achieved, all those great wars, all that human slaughter and bloodshed'.[8] This is in my view a much too moralistic objection. As a matter of fact, English is rapidly coming to fulfil the role that Latin once played and is now our *lingua franca*. Viewed *sub specie aeternitatis*, this may seem less than desirable, it may be correctly interpreted as a sign of Anglo-American imperialism and it has certainly had a cost in terms of slaughter and bloodshed and yet, being a fact, it means that this kind of objection to a global citizenship loses its force.

Of course, the use of English as a second language has not yet spread round the entire globe. If its further spread requires *more* warfare and bloodshed, then, of course, it might be a good idea not to rely on the use of English in the future. There is, however, little evidence to indicate that warfare is a causal mechanism when English spreads around the globe *today*, irrespective of what the causes were in the past. Today the spread of English takes place through cultural institutions, mass media and science rather than through warfare, and I see no problem with that.

4. Lack of economic integration

An economic objection, similar to the communitarian one, but based on the concern that there is lack of *economic* unification in the world rather than ethnic or cultural, has been put forward. These critics claim, advocates of economic globalisation notwithstanding, that existing economic development does not point in the direction of true integration – economic development means widening gaps and many are simply left behind. As Danilo Zolo puts the point:

> The rhetoric of civil globalization and of a rising 'cosmopolitan citizenship' underestimates one of the most characteristic and

most serious consequences of the way in which westernization is cultural homogenization without integration: namely, the antagonism between the esteemed citizenships of the West and the countless masses belonging to regional and subcontinental areas without development and with a high rate of demographic growth ... And all signs point to a worsening of the situation over the coming decades.[9]

This is somewhat exaggerated. At least the part about a high rate of demographic growth doesn't seem to fit the picture any more. According to received wisdom today, it is thought that the global population will stabilise around the year 2050 (at a high level creating environmental problems, to be certain). And we have seen, in Chapter 3, that it is difficult to say with good grounds anything definite about the recent economic trends in the world. However, we did see that there is no ground for the claim that we are approaching global equality; quite the contrary, the present (highly unequal) situation seems to be rather stable and the absolute differences are bound to increase for a long time ahead of us. Even more importantly, as we also saw in Chapter 3, in sixteen of the world's poorest countries average per capita income has actually fallen.[10] So, even if exaggerated, Zolo's main point seems to be correct. There is no true economic integration in our world, at least not in the sense that all peoples are, or are rapidly becoming, involved in the economy on equal terms. But is this a good argument against the attempt to establish global democracy? I think not.

What Zolo points to are the undesirable consequences of the existing economic development, not consequences of any cosmopolitan citizenship as such. On the contrary, what Zolo points to could rather be seen as good arguments as to why we should attempt to establish global democracy.

It is crucial to find strategies that improve the economic situation in the world, but there is no reason to think that a cosmopolitan citizenship would in itself prove problematic to such a desired development. On the contrary, to the extent that it can be democratised, in the manner discussed above, there are good reasons to believe that it will be one among many possible instruments to a better development of all sorts of aspects of the world. Once again the means to global justice is not redistributive global taxes on an individual level, but political measures designed to empower poor people themselves all over the world to improve their own lot. We have seen that a world government is a *sine qua non*, not an obstacle, if we want to move in this direction. In particular, it is important to observe that, just as the establishment of a cosmopolitan citizenship does not presuppose the existence of cultural homogeneity, it does not presuppose any existing economic integration. The former is probably not desirable, the latter is, but neither is a prerequisite to the establishment of a cosmopolitan citizenship.

Even a dedicated socialist, like myself, should admit that the establishment of global democracy is one thing, the establishment of global justice quite another, and the latter should not be allowed to stand in the way of the former. I do believe, and I have stressed this before, that it would be helpful if socialism could be established in many nation-states, perhaps along the lines given by David Schweickart in his book *After Capitalism*, earlier discussed in this book, or in some other form; this would render easier the elimination of global injustices. But this does not mean that it would be a good idea to put off the struggle for global democracy while we wait for socialism.

5. Shared sovereignty

I noted at the beginning of the book that three approaches compete with regard to how we ought to handle global problems. I argued that we should attempt to establish global democracy. Global democracy can solve problems to do with peace, justice and a good environment, but the idea that we can solve them without giving up national sovereignty proved to be a non-starter. I have not, however, yet discussed the problem of whether it would be possible only partially to do so. Why not opt for a kind of hybrid solution, where national sovereignty is given up with respect to some issues, but not with respect to others? I now turn to a critical examination of this idea.

Some want to opt for a compromise position, then, which I have referred to as a hybrid. In this view, we may well have a kind of world government, but it should not be sovereign: there should be a system of *shared* sovereignty between the world government and nation-states. So I had better address this question: should the world parliament be sovereign?

It needs to be sovereign. It is tempting to argue that once international and national affairs have been properly separated, it is enough if the world parliament decides about international affairs.[11] However, in the view of cosmopolitan democracy I here defend, it is crucial that the world parliament is sovereign. It, and it alone, decides on what level a certain decision should be taken.

Here I am in disagreement with most other cosmopolitan writers who opt for a kind of hybrid solution rather than a true federation.[12] This is true of many 'classical' statements of a cosmopolitan view, relying on the distinction between national and international affairs, such as those put forward by the World Movement for World Federal Government at the end of the Second World War, requiring merely that 'limitations' of national sovereignty be made and urging merely that the transfer to the world federal government should take place of such legislative, executive and judicial powers as 'relate' to world affairs.[13] Once other reasons for world government, besides securing a lasting peace, have been added more complicated demarcation problems have surfaced. Recent examples of such confederate rather than truly federate views are hence cast in more complex terms. One such view is exemplified by the Italian cosmopolitan thinker Daniele Archibugi who states that:

> democratic procedures and norms need to be tailored according to the issues concerned: for example, what are the appropriate constituencies to settle problems involving two local communities of separate states but located on opposite sides of the same river, for problems involving regional settlements, or for problems of global concern? Quite clearly, the forum will be different in each of these cases.[14]

An even more elaborate proposal in the same vein has been put forward by the contemporary British cosmopolitan thinker David Held who hesitates to propose that the sovereignty of the world parliament be exchanged for the (lost) sovereignty of national states (parliaments). Like Archibugi he is not satisfied with any simplistic division of questions into national and international and he proposes a complex system for distributing authority to different levels with regard to different issues. This is how he describes the system:

> The test of extensiveness examines the range of peoples within and across delimited territories who are significantly affected by a collective problem and policy question. The test of intensity assesses the degree to which the latter impinges on a group of people(s) and, therefore, the degree to which national, regional or global legislation or other types of intervention are justified. The third test, the assessment of comparative efficiency, is concerned to provide a means of examining whether any proposed national, regional or global initiative is necessary in so far as the objectives it seeks to meet cannot be realised in an adequate way by those operating at 'lower' levels of decision-making.[15]

Let me give just one more example. This is an example of some importance. Few people seem to realise that the Catholic Church, through Pope John XXIII in his *Pacem in Terris*, has advocated a cosmopolitan solution to the problem of world peace:

> the common good of all nations involves problems which affect people all the world over: problems which can only be solved by a public authority ... whose writ covers the entire globe. We cannot therefore escape the conclusion that the moral order itself demands the establishment of some sort of world government.[16]

The Pope, of course, advocates the principle of 'subsidiarity', according to which decisions should be taken at the lowest possible level, positing a hierarchical socio-political structure. This idea is well-known from the horizon of the European Union, where it has become accepted policy.

I would have none of this, however. I do not deny that different questions should be handled at different levels, of course, and I concede that existing states in most cases should continue to exist when a world government is established. Indeed, I share the view that few problems should be actually dealt with on a global level. Here mainly problems to do with peace, justice and a good environment should be addressed. However, I do claim that in the transition to a world government these states must be robbed entirely of their *sovereignty*. They become, once the world parliament is in place, similar to local governments within a nation-state. The right they have to decide is held because this is how power has been delegated from the highest level downwards.

The reason for this radicalism is simple. No algorithm assigning decisions to the appropriate level can be provided. The idea that those who are affected by a decision should take it is far too vague to be of much help. And it gets even worse if we also have to assess to what extent those affected are affected. This means that, nice as it may sound, the 'all affected principle', or the 'subsidiary' principle becomes useless for the purpose of 'limiting' national sovereignty. We have also seen that, taken literally, no one seems to want to adhere to the 'all affected' principle, since we want people to have dictatorial power over certain decisions; in particular this is true of their decisions about how to act, vote and manage their personal belongings. Moreover, the old distinction between national and international affairs is extremely vague, politically contested and insufficient when it comes to problems to do not only with war and peace, but also with the environment, international justice and so forth. Various different political ideologies will answer the question to which level a certain decision belongs differently. Yet there must be a definite place where the questions are sorted into appropriate levels.

Suppose there is conflict, and conflict there will be. Unless there are sanctions available to the central authority to back up a decision as to where a question is to be handled, the system of states will be thrown back into a state of nature. Rousseau was right in his claim that sovereignty is indivisible.[17] Note that this was a descriptive claim, not a normative one. For an illustration of the difficulty of establishing a system of shared sovereignty the European situation should be considered. When strong powers such as France and Germany have flouted common economic decisions, in particular the Stability Pact, allowing deficits at variance with the EU regulations, there has been no way for the rest of the Member States to force them into compliance. It is my suggestion that it is up to the central political authority, the world government, to decide where a question should be handled. Here radicalism is once again the key to realism.

6. Totalitarian spectre

A final objection to the idea of a sovereign world government is that it might become tyrannical. After all, when we establish a world government, if we do, this is a single shot. When a national democratic government is established the result may turn out to be devastating. We know from the Weimar republic that a people may come to elect a dictator as its ruler. What if something similar happened on a global scale? In particular, if a centralised military force is established and put in the hands of the world government, does this not mean that the world government itself might come to pose a totalitarian threat to the world? Would it not be, if it could be established, an unprecedented almighty and terrible force? Would it not be safer to follow the advice of Immanuel Kant (followed up in the twentieth century by Hans Kelsen and John Rawls)[18] and opt rather for an association of independent states? This is how Kant himself puts forward his concerns:

> The idea of a law of nations presupposes the separate existence of many states which are independent of each other. Such a situation constitutes in and by itself a state of war (unless there is a federal union to prevent hostilities breaking out). Yet

such a situation is from the standpoint of reason better than the complete merging of all these states in one ... because the laws lose more and more of their effectiveness as the government increases in size, and the resulting soulless despotism is plunged into anarchy after having exterminated all the germs of good.[19]

It may seem here as though Kant accepts the federal solution to the problem of maintaining international peace but, as was pointed out in previous chapters, appearances are deceptive. What Kant has in mind when he speaks of a 'federal union' is a union of 'free states'. What he means by 'federation' is not what is here meant by the word. Rather what Kant hopes for is peaceful cooperation between separate states and this, I believe, is utopian. He may even himself be aware of this when he speaks of his system as a ultimately a 'state of war'. Yet, for all that, he wants to stick with this basic kind of system, tempered merely through voluntary and temporary treaties between free states.

Why? Obviously not only because he thinks the idea of a world government utopian but also, and mainly, because he does not see it as desirable. So his objection needs to be discussed. The objection comes in two parts. First, we have the objection that a world government must result in soulless despotism. This view is founded on a misunderstanding, at least when the objection is directed at the kind of proposal I have made here. The military force of a world government need not, and should not, be a particularly strong one. If it were, then the United States would not feel any inclination to surrender to it! The UN force need only be sufficiently strong to contain terrorist groups and to secure peace and order, but no stronger than this. The American military supremacy will not, and ought not, be challenged by the world government. The reason that the United States eventually surrenders to it, if it does, must be because there seems to be no further point in it carrying the economic burden of maintaining a military force of the kind with which we are familiar today. In a world where security is guaranteed by the UN, and where neither the UN nor any other power challenges American military supremacy, there would be no need for the vast United States military.

What about the second part of Kant's objection, then, the part that says 'laws lose more and more of their effectiveness as the government increases in size'? This may be true of some laws, but hopefully the world parliament will not pass that kind of bill. However, with respect to other kinds of laws, the opposite is true. We saw this in the opening chapters of this book. With respect to peace, justice and the environment nothing short of global legislation will be effective.

Take, for example, restrictions intended to counter global warming. We know that it is difficult for free states to solve this kind of problem. They immediately find themselves facing the problem of the tragedy of the commons. Each nation-state has good egoistic reasons to go on with their own emissions, even though each wants the others to have a cap on theirs. This is true irrespective of how bad the global situation becomes, and it is unlikely that an altruistic concern for our shared well-being on the globe will be forthcoming. So here the only efficient manner of legislating is to legislate for the entire globe. I will not go into this once again, it has been effectively dealt with in Chapters 2 to 4.

This is not to say that a cosmopolitan democracy as a political system is foolproof, of course. What if the world parliament doesn't rest satisfied with the kind of problems for which it has been devised? After all, it is sovereign, so, in principle, it can start to meddle with the lives of the world's citizens as it sees fit. In particular, the world parliament could come to be taken over by fundamentalists of some sort and the military forces at the command of the world government may be used for oppressive purposes. We seem to be back, then, to Kant's concern about despotism, if not in a 'soulless' form, so rather in an only *too* 'soulful' one.

I have argued repeatedly that the global democracy *should* confine itself to problems to do with peace, global justice and the environment, and to treat these problems in a cautious manner. In the chapter on democracy, I *assumed* that this would be how the world government would behave. Given this assumption I argued that it would be effective in handling the global problems facing humanity. Now the time has come to question this assumption. After all, I have also argued that there is no way of drawing a *principled* line between questions with which the global democracy should, and questions with which it should not, deal. I have argued that the world parliament must be sovereign. Does this not mean that, if we choose to establish it, we leave our destiny in the hands of a highly dangerous Leviathan?

There is no denying that we do. Moreover, no political system is foolproof. However, the situation is in a way more hopeful when it comes to a world government than when it comes to any national government in particular. The more all-encompassing a system is, the less serious the risk that it will be taken over by one very special factional interest. So even if a system of world government is special in the sense that its establishment is a matter of a 'single shot', this is a shot to be looked upon with more optimism than any one levelled before, on a restricted national level.

There is no radical and very special religious belief, nor any political belief of the same radical order in the world today that seems capable of commanding allegiance from more than a tiny fraction of the world's population. A fundamentalist religion can conquer a state and even a region of the world, but hardly the entire globe. This should be our source of hope and confidence in the prospects of cosmopolitan democracy. As a matter of fact, my own fear is not that the world parliament, besides dealing with the problems it was designed to solve, will be too eager to solve all sorts of problems. My fear is rather that, with respect to the problems it is really there to solve, it will be only too complacent in order not to meddle with local habits and cultural practices.

However, even if it is not likely that the world parliament will be taken over by any fundamentalist religion in particular, there is a definite risk that representatives of many different dogmatic and fundamental religions could get together and try to impose illiberal laws on the world. Something that might substantiate such a concern is a much publicised event which took place only a few years ago. It created not only media hype all over the world, but also demonstrations and riots with casualties in some places of the world. I refer to the publication in a Danish newspaper, *Jyllands-Posten*, of some satirical cartoons which offended fundamentalist Muslims all over the world. Although this story will soon be forgotten, one result of it may remain. Newspapers may become more cautious when it comes to publishing things that may offend some people on the globe.

The fact that it is possible to cause offence in this manner is due to globalisation as such. It is characteristic of globalisation that many societies contain within themselves populations with different religions; and globalisation also engenders the fact that societies with different populations adhering to different religions communicate more intimately with one another. In a global *democracy*, where people with different religions and cultures live even closer to one another, the tendency to self-censorship would probably be even stronger.

Here it is not only self-censorship that we must fear. For even if there is no risk that one particular religion will gain the upper hand in the world parliament and force itself upon people all over the globe, there is, as we have seen, a definite risk that the representatives of *different* religions *together* will vote for laws that are illiberal with respect to the press and other media. We can see one example of this kind of tendency in a resolution in 2007 at the UN Human Rights Council urging a global prohibition on the public defamation of religion – a response largely to the furore over the caricatures published in a Danish newspaper of the Prophet Muhammad. Although this resolution has no legal force, once a world parliament is in place, laws to the same effect, *with* legal force, *may* come to be passed.

This may be the price we have to pay, at least for a considerable time, while reaping the fruits of global democracy. A comforting fact is, however, that, in a world marked by globalisation, there exist many informal ways for people to communicate their views to each other without using public media that can be submitted to public censorship. So much of the rationale behind the freedom of the press can probably be retained as, certainly, electronic communication will be of growing political importance in a globalised world, with or without global democracy.

I have earlier indicated that I am sceptical of a system of judicial review. However, many people do not share my scepticism. They may find that, if a global high court is in place, capable of striking down illiberal laws, they will feel more comfortable with the existence of a world government and a global democracy. So perhaps, if a system of judicial review is introduced in order to facilitate the step from a situation where big and influential nations have a veto against decisions taken by the world government, there may still be reasons to retain it, once the global democracy is in place.

Be that as it may, if my conjecture is borne out by realities, the existence of one global democracy need not mean that there will be no room for local variations. Quite the contrary. If the world government, in an attempt to further global justice through empowerment of people locally, stops transnational enterprises from blackmailing local governments, then there will be less pressure in the direction of levelling out cultural differences locally. As a matter of fact, there will be plenty of room, not only for differences, but also for social experiments where quite different local, national and regional political and cultural traditions are, in a manner of speaking, being put to the test. And this would mean that, even if there is no way for dissatisfied world citizens to emigrate from the global community, there will be plenty of room for migrations between different local and national communities. Once problems to do with war, justice and the environment have been solved, more open attitudes to migrants all over the world are likely to evolve.

8
Conclusion

There is no denying that many problems facing humanity are global in nature. If we are to solve them at all, we need to solve them on a global level. This is probably true of problems to do with war and peace. This is true also of problems to do with global justice. And it is obviously true also of problems to do with the environment. These problems cannot be solved within nation-states, they need to be solved on a global level. How could this be achieved? There seem to be three main ideas about this.

One possible response to global problems is to stick to national democracy and attempt to keep various different forms of trans-national and cosmopolitan citizenships 'as thin as possible'. The global problems should be solved through peaceful cooperation between sovereign and civilised states. It has been contended that once the individual states become democratised, they will no more wage war against one another. And once individually they adopt just welfare institutions and redistributive schemes, they will also provide some support to those in need. Finally, once they become democratised and, economically speaking more equal, they will agree on treaties putting a stop to the waste of scarce resources and the spread of dangerous stuffs.

Is this realistic? I have gone to considerable lengths to show that it is not. Even democracies may wage war against one another, and, in

Conclusion

the absence of a global democracy, there is no guarantee that democracy will spread around the world. In fact, powerful democracies, when they see fit, may come to block the road to democracy in some parts of the world and even overthrow established democracies. And even democratic national governments may be drawn into a competition for goodwill from transnational corporations, 'selling out' human rights and decent working conditions in exchange for investment. Even socialist states may feel a strong temptation to do so. Finally, in relation to environmental problems, even democratic governments will come to face many tragedies of the commons. The recent problem with global warming seems to be an example of this: it is reasonable to assume that there is more to come in the future.

Moreover, many people today seem to believe that globalisation poses a threat to national democracy. This means that, to the extent that we think democracy is necessary to the solution of some global problems – to obviate war, for example – we may be in a situation where there is no democratic alternative to global democracy. We simply have to exchange one flourishing global democracy for many withering national ones. As we remember, former United Nations Secretary-General Boutros Boutros-Ghali, among many others, has voiced this concern when he states that:

> We need to promote the democratization of globalization, before globalization destroys the foundations of national and international democracy.[1]

Another possible response, if we do not want to go for global democracy, would be to go for a hybrid solution. Each problem should be solved at the level where it can be best handled. To which level a certain problem belongs must be decided through negotiation between states, giving up some, but not all, of their sovereignty by signing binding treaties.

I have dismissed this merely theoretical possibility as, indeed, unrealistic in practice. Rousseau seems to be right in his insistence that sovereignty is indivisible. Unless nation-states give up their sovereignty altogether to the global institutions there will be different opinions as to where various questions belong. Unless such differences of opinion can be sorted out at the highest possible level, they will not be sorted out at all. The global system will be thrown back into anarchy.

If my argument is correct, then, we have to bear with war, global injustice and a poor environment unless we resort to a world government. The options are more radical than many in the contemporary discussion about globalisation have admitted. Even if it seems plausible to assume that a world government would be able to deal with problems to do with war, injustice and the environment, it might be questioned both whether a world government is possible and whether it is desirable.

I have answered both these questions in the affirmative by arguing that a world government is possible and desirable, provided it takes a radical populist democratic shape. What should be established is global democracy.

My argument to the effect that global democracy is possible has taken the form of a road map in its direction, starting with rather small steps, relying on a tendency towards democratic determinism, eventually leading in the right direction. Two processes are here crucial, and it is crucial that they are run in tandem: democratisation of the UN; and successive military capitulation from nation-states in relation to the UN.

It is interesting to note that, irrespective of whether one likes the idea of global democracy, these two initial steps may each seem very attractive in themselves. Just imagine the possibilities if there had been a global, directly elected Peoples' Assembly that could have discussed the problem of global warming, capable of deciding about at least recommendations for global action. There is no denying that this also would have been helpful when it comes to reaching international agreements. Or, imagine that there had been military forces readily at the disposal of a Security Council intent on handling the Darfur conflict.

The only reason for rejecting the two first steps here indicated as parts of the road map, then, must be that adopting them might set us on a slippery slope, leading all the way to a full blown world government. If you like the idea as such of global democracy, you are bound to be enthusiastic with respect to these steps.

I have argued that the presence of one only superpower is a favourable condition to this endeavour. The final step, I have conjectured, would be when the United States surrenders its military forces to the UN. The United States should be cajoled and shamed by the rest of the world to the point where surrender is irresistible.

But is global democracy desirable? Even if it is a means to the solution of some pressing global problems, global democracy might be considered so terrible in itself that we would be better bearing with war, injustice and environmental disasters. This is hard to believe. Moreover, even if there exists a sceptical tradition with respect to world government dating back at least to Immanuel Kant, and followed up in the twentieth century by thinkers such as Hans Kelsen and John Rawls, I have tried to show that global democracy is highly desirable.

Against the charges that such a democracy would be shallow (few and restricted options will be open to it), that in its early stages it will be in the grips of the government of the United States, it has been objected that, even if this is so, there is a potential for institutions such as a world parliament to grow more important as well as more independent in the future. Meanwhile, the world is, anyway, in the grips of the United States government.

Against the charges that there is a lack of cultural and ethnic community necessary for political unity on the globe, I have argued that such community is not desirable even on a national level, let alone on a global level. Or, to the extent that it is necessary on a national scale, in order to render possible redistributive tax systems, we need not resort to it on the global level. This has to do with the fact that global injustices should be attacked, not through redistribution between individuals on the globe, but, mainly, through laws empowering poor people across the entire world, allowing them by themselves to better their own situation.

Against the charges that a global political democracy may evolve into tyranny (of the majority over the minority) it has been claimed that, even if there is no guarantee to the opposite effect, the more all-encompassing a polity is, the less serious this risk becomes. And it is difficult to think of a polity that is more all-encompassing than the world itself.

Finally, provided world government is possible and desirable, how may it come about? In the same manner that national democracy has come about, where it has, I have argued: through political struggle.

People who feel that they are already world citizens must take the lead. They must articulate political programmes, organise worldwide political campaigns, steam up the political process and get it in motion. New media render this kind of political action not only possible but also almost inevitable. Once only a few steps have been taken in the right direction democratic determinism will start to operate.

Or so I hope, at any rate.

Notes

Preface

1 H. G. Wells, *Imperialism and the Open Conspiracy* (London: Faber & Faber, 1929).
2 Accessed on 6 November, 2005: http://www.newint.org/issue289/xword.htm.
3 See, for example, Richard Falk and Andrew Strauss, 'On the creation of a global peoples' assembly: legitimacy and the power of popular sovereignty', *Stanford Journal of International Law* (2000), 36: 191–220. See also http://en.unpacampaign.org/appeal/ for a growing global political initiative urging that a parliamentary assembly should be added to the United Nations.
4 Media Release – Friday, 18 May 2007 from the Secretariat of the Campaign for a United Nations Parliamentary Assembly.
5 Media Release – Friday, 18 May 2007.

Chapter 1

1 The pioneers seem to have been Emeric Crucé with his *Noveau Cynée* (1623–4) followed by Anacharsis Cloots, *La Rêpublique universelle* at the time of the French Revolution (1792).
2 Others have opted for a 'technocratic' version, most famously H. G. Wells, in a series of books published between 1901 and 1940, ranging from *Anticipations* (London: Chapman & Hall, 1901) to *The Common Sense of War and Peace* (Harmondsworth: Penguin, 1940).

Chapter 2

1 Hans Kelsen, *Peace Through Law* (Chapel Hill, NC: University of North Carolina Press, 1944), pp. 5–6.
2 On 20 November 1948, in a public speech. The exact details about what he said are, however, contested. Nicholas Griffin of McMaster University, in his book *The Selected Letters of Bertrand Russell: The Public Years, 1914–1970* (New York: Routledge, 1992), has claimed that Russell's wording implies he didn't advocate the actual use of the atom bomb, but merely its diplomatic use as a massive source of leverage over the actions of the Soviets.
3 Immanuel Kant, *Perpetual Peace and Other Essays* (Indianapolis, IN: Hacket, 1983), pp. 112–13 (emphasis original).

4 Kant, *Perpetual Peace*, p. 117.
5 Kant, *Perpetual Peace*, pp. 117–18.
6 Kant, *Perpetual Peace*, p. 113.
7 *Human Security Report* (Oxford: Oxford University Press, 2005), available at http://www.humansecurityreport.info/, accessed on 27 January 2006.
8 J. Glover, *Humanity: A Moral History of the Twentieth Century* (London: Jonathan Cape, 1999), p. 1.
9 *Human Security Report* (2005).
10 *Human Security Report* (2005).
11 R. J. Rummel, *Power Kills: Democracy as a Method of Nonviolence* (New Brunswick, NJ: Transaction Publishers, 1997).
12 The interview was published in *Peace Magazine*, May–June 1999, p. 10, and it is also accessible at: http://www.peacemagazine.org/archive/v15n3p10.htm.
13 Gustaf Arrhenius has reminded me of this example.
14 John Norton Moore, 'Editorial comments: "Solving the war puzzle"', *American Journal of International Law* (2003), 97(2): 2882, 2840.
15 Rummel, *Power Kills*.
16 Rummel, *Power Kills*.
17 *Human Security Report* (2005).
18 H. Bull, *The Anarchial Society* (London: Macmillan, 1977), pp. 254–5.
19 J. D. Faeron and D. D. Laitin, 'Ethnicity, insurgency, and civil war', *American Political Science Review* (2003), 97: 75–90; E. N. Muller and E. Weede, 'Cross-national variations in political violence: a rational action approach', *Journal of Conflict Resolution* (1990), 34: 624–51. Hegre *et al.*, 'Toward a democratic civil peace?', *American Political Science Review* (2001), 95: 33–48.
20 *Human Security Report* (2005).
21 *Human Security Report* (2005).
22 The new Uppsala/Human Security Centre dataset shows that the number of conflicts in Africa in which a government was one of the warring parties declined from fifteen to ten between 2002 and 2003. The number of cases of 'one-sided' violence – defined as the slaughter of at least twenty-five civilians in the course of a year and called one-sided because the victims cannot fight back – declined from seventeen to eleven, a drop of 35 per cent. Meanwhile, reported fatalities from all forms of political violence were down by more than 24 per cent: *Human Security Report* (2005).

Chapter 3

1 I have these health statistics from James Dwyer, 'Global health justice', *Bioethics* (2005), 19: 460–75.
2 Can a measurement of well-being be constructed such that the utilitarian claim becomes meaningful? It can, I have argued elsewhere, at least in principle. It is difficult to measure well-being in practice, of course, but with

Notes

respect to different alternatives facing an agent; it makes sense, hence, to say that an alternative in a situation is right. This claim is either true or false. See T. Tannsjo, *Hedonistic Utilitarianism* (Edinburgh: Edinburgh University Press, 1998), with reference to this.

3 A. Melchior, K. Telle and H. Wiig, 'Globalisation and inequality' (Oslo: Royal Norwegian Ministry of Foreign Affairs, 2000), pp. l 16–17, 21.
4 P. Svedberg, 'World income distributions: which way?', *Journal of Development Studies* (2004), 40(5): 25.
5 J. Locke, *Second Treatise of Government*, section 27.
6 R. Nozick, *Anarchy, State, and Utopia* (Oxford: Blackwell, 1974), p. 178.
7 H. L. A. Hart, *The Concept of Law*, 2nd edn (Oxford: Oxford University Press, 1994).
8 J. Rawls, *A Theory of Justice* (Cambridge, MA: Harvard University Press, 1971), note 8, p. 303.
9 John Rawls, *The Law of Peoples* (Cambridge, MA: Harvard University Press, 1999), p. 37.
10 Rawls, *The Law of Peoples*, p. 36.
11 There exist other interesting attempts in the same vein; see also, for example, Hillel Steiner, 'Just taxation and international redistribution', in I. Shapiro and L. Brilmayer (eds), *Global Justice* (New York: New York University Press, 1999).
12 T. W. Pogge, 'An egalitarian law of peoples', *Philosophy and Public Affairs* (1994) 23: 195–224 at 199.
13 In an earlier paper 'Cosmopolitanism and sovereignty', *Ethics* (1992), 103: 48–75, Pogge defended what I have here called a compromise position, where sovereignty is vertically dispersed. In Chapter 7 I discuss and reject this kind of idea. I there defend the idea that sovereignty is indivisible.
14 Pogge, 'An egalitarian law of peoples', p. 219.
15 Pogge, 'An egalitarian law of peoples', p. 204.
16 Pogge, 'An egalitarian law of peoples', p. 203.
17 Pogge, 'An egalitarian law of peoples', pp. 202–3.
18 P. Singer, *One World. The Ethics of Globalization* (New Haven, CT: Yale University Press, 2002).
19 P. Unger, *Living High and Letting Die. Our Illusion of Innocence* (Oxford: Oxford University Press).
20 See D. Miller, *Citizenship and National Identity* (Cambridge: Polity Press, 2000), for an elaboration (and, indeed, overstatement) of this point. Both Kai Nielsen and Gillian Brock have argued in correspondence and conversation, respectively, that I am too optimistic with respect to achieving global justice without much redistribution. If this is true, then I am afraid this means that global democracy is less efficient when it comes to dealing with problems of global injustices than I have argued. It is hard to believe that the communitarians are wrong on *this* point.

21 The quotation is from Andre Gunder Frank, *Dependent Accumulation and Underdevelopment* (New York: Monthly Review Press, 1979), pp. 98–9, also quoted by D. Schweickart, *After Capitalism* (Lanham, MD: Rowman & Littlefield, 2002), p. 78.

22 I will return to this problem when, in a forthcoming chapter, I draw up my road map to global democracy.

Chapter 4

1 I have the statistics from chapter 2 of Peter Singer's *One World*. He carefully quotes the original sources. There is no need for me to go into details here.

2 Singer, *One World*.

3 http://www.ipcc.ch/SPM2feb07.pdf, accessed 19 February 2007.

4 http://www.ipcc.ch/SPM2fed07.pdf.

5 Singer, *One World*, p. 26.

6 Interview in the leading Swedish daily newspaper, *Dagens Nyheter*, on 2 February 2007.

7 http://www.publicintegrity.org/default.aspx, accessed on 2 September 2005.

8 http://www.publicintegrity.org.

9 The problem was famously named by Garrett Hardin, 'The tragedy of the commons', *Science* (1968), 162: 1243–8.

10 In particular, this is a position defended by the Association for the Study of Peak Oil & Gas, which argues that many of the prophecies about problems in relation to global warming will not come true since they rely on overly optimistic assessments of the oil and gas resources. They claim that before we have produced all the bad effects, the oil and gas resources will be used up. Information about their assessments can be found at: http://www.peakoil.net/contact.html.

11 *Arizona Water Resource* (Nov.–Dec. 1999), 8(3), also on the net at http://ag.arizona.edu/AZWATER/awr/dec99/Feature2.htm, accessed 10 November 2005.

12 *Arizona Water Resource*.

13 The best defence of this view I know of is given in Arne Naess, *Ecology, Community and Lifestyle: Outline of an Ecosophy* (Cambridge: Cambridge University Press, 1989).

14 http://www.signonsandiego.com/news/world/20040915-0612-environment-japan-whaling.html, accessed on 1 November 2005.

Chapter 5

1 The counterfactual clause is used to counter objections to the effect that Condorcet or Arrow has shown that a 'populist' notion of democracy, resting on the idea that a majority will should be decisive, is flawed. Cf. William Riker, *Liberalism Against Populism: A Confrontation Between the Theory of*

Notes

Democracy and the Theory of Social Choice (San Francisco, CA: Freeman, 1982), for the most influential statement of objections of the kind.

2 See K. J. Arrow, *Social Choice and Individual Values* (New York: Wiley, 1951).

3 I owe this way of putting the point to Lars Bergström.

4 J. Madison, *The Federalist Papers* (New York: Doubleday, 1966), No. 10, p. 20.

5 John Adams, 'Letter to John Penn', p. 205. Here quoted from Hanna Pitkin, *The Concept of Representation* (Berkeley, CA: University of California Press, 1967), p. 60.

6 Joseph Schumpeter, *Capitalism, Socialism, and Democracy* (London: Unwin, 1943), pp. 173–4.

7 John S. Dryzek, *Deliberative Democracy and Beyond. Liberals, Critics, Contestations* (Oxford: Oxford University Press, 2000), p. v.

8 For a defence of a similar, even more pessimistic view, see Cass R. Sunstein, *Republic.com* (Princeton, NJ: Princeton University Press, 2001).

9 For a more optimistic assessment, see James Fishkin, *The Voice of the People: Public Opinion and Democracy* (New Haven, CT: Yale University Press, 1995).

10 It can be accessed at http://en.unpacampaign.org/appeal.

11 Dryzek, *Deliberative Democracy*, p. 3.

12 D. Black, 'On the rationale of group decision-making', *Journal of Political Economy* (1948), 56: 23–34.

13 For a recent discussion on the epistemic idea of democracy, see W. Rabinowicz and L. Bovens, 'Democratic answers to complex questions – an epistemic perspective', in M. Sintonen (ed.), *Socratic Method of Questioning as Philosophy and as Method* (Dordrecht: Kluwer, 2004).

14 For a defence of such a model, see H. Brighouse and M. Fleurbaey, 'On the fair allocation of power' (Mimeo, 2005).

15 In my book, *Populist Democracy*, I discuss this model as well.

16 This is the theme of a research project at the Department of Philosophy, Stockholm University. For a statement of some of the problems with democracy as a protection against the suppression of the majority by a minority, see my 'Rational injustice', *Philosophy of the Social Sciences* (2006), 36: 423–39.

17 The objection has been made by an anonymous reviewer for Edinburgh University Press on my manuscript.

18 Anonymous Edinburgh University Press reviewer on my manuscript.

19 A. Bickel, *The Least Dangerous Branch* (Indianapolis, IN: Bobbs-Merrill, 1962), pp. 16–17.

20 For a defence of the received wisdom in the United States, see John Hart Eley, *Democracy and Distrust — A Theory of Judicial Review* (Cambridge, MA: Harvard University Press, 1980). For a critical evaluation of the system of judicial review, see Robert Dahl's 1957 article 'Decision-making in a democracy: the supreme court as a national policy maker'.

21 Here quoted from Wikipedia http://en.wikipedia.org/wiki/Judicial_review, accessed 7 November 2006.

Chapter 6

 1 Brian Barry, 'Statism and nationalism: a cosmopolitan critique', in I. Shapiro and L. Brilmayer (eds), *Global Justice* (New York: New York University Press, 1999), p. 35.
 2 In Chapter 1 I mentioned Crucé with his pioneering work in 1623–4. It seems as if this theme has been raised over and over again at the end of devastating wars. One such discussion was conducted at the end of the First World War, resulting in the creation of the League of Nations. After the Second World War the discussion was intense with contributions from distinguished thinkers such as Kelsen and A. C. Ewing. My own interest in the subject was raised at the end of the Cold War. The number of other recent proposals is legion: to mention only a few examples, see J. Burnheim, *Is Democracy Possible?* (Cambridge: Polity Press, 1985); D. Held, *Democracy and the Global Order. From the Modern State to Cosmopolitan Governance* (Cambridge: Polity Press, 1995); and Nigel Dower, *An Introduction to Global Citizenship* (Edingburgh: Edinburgh University Press, 2003). Many people in recent times, such as Johan Galtung, for example, have been rather specific concerning reforms of the UN institutions. For a comprehensive statement of his view, see 'Alternative models for global democracy', in B. Holden (ed.), *Global Democracy. Key Debates* (London: Routledge, 2000).
 3 A. C. Ewing, *The Individual, the State, and World Government* (New York: Macmillian, 1947), p. 289.
 4 J. Galtung, 'Alternative models for global democracy', p. 154.
 5 T. Hobbes, *Leviathan* (Oxford: Oxford University Press, [1651] 1996), Part 2, chapter XVII, 2.
 6 http://www.thechicagocouncil.org/dynamic_page.php?id=61, accessed 18 May 2007.
 7 A. C. Ewing, *The Individual, the State, and World Government*, pp. 294–5.
 8 http://www.atimes.com/atimes/China_Business/GL08Cb05.html, accessed on 22 August 2006.
 9 P. Svedberg, 'World income distribution: which way?', *Journal of Development Studies* (2004), 40: 19–20.
10 See his blog, at http://www.becker-posner-blog.com/archives /2005/04/will_china_beco.html, accessed on 25 August 2006.
11 Ibid.
12 *Armaments, Disarmaments and International Security: SIPRI Yearbook 2007* (Stockholm: Stockholm International Peace Institute, 2007).
13 In an essay written by Habermas, co-signed by Derrida, published in the *Frankfurter Allgemeine Zeitung* in June 2003. The authors advocate a strong European Union capable of challenging the United States even in military

terms. Certainly, they are not the first thinkers to develop this theme; it was taken up in 1866 by Michael Chevalier, who supported the establishment of the United States of Europe as a counter-weight to the American 'political colossus' that was emerging on the other side of the Atlantic. See F. H. Hinsley, *Power and the Pursuit of Peace* (Cambridge: Cambridge University Press, 1963), p. 122 about this.

14 D. Beetham, *Democracy: A Beginner's Guide* (Oxford: Oneworld, 2005), p. 55.

15 See in particular the seminal book by D. Acemoglu and J. Robinson, *Economic Origins of Dictatorship and Democracy* (Cambridge: Cambridge University Press, 2006). Their main hypothesis was anticipated in 1971 by Robert Dahl, *Polyarchy: Participation and Opposition* (New Haven, CT: Yale University Press, 1971).

Chapter 7

1 I rely here mainly on Daron Acemoglu and James A. Robinson, *Economic Origins of Dictatorship and Democracy*.

2 See, for example, A. MacIntyre, *Whose Justice? Which Rationality?* (Notre Dame, IN: Univeristy of Notre Dame Press, 1991); M. Sandel, *Liberalism and the Limits of Justice*, 2nd edn (Cambridge: Cambridge University Press, 1998); C. Taylor, 'Conditions of an unforced consensus on human rights', in J. R. Bauer and D. Bell (eds), *The East Asian Challenge for Human Rights* (New York: Cambridge University Press, 1999); and M. Walzer, *Thick and Thin* (Notre Dame, IN: Notre Dame University Press, 1994).

3 Will Kymlicka, *Politics in the Vernacular: Nationalism, Multiculturalism, and Citizenship* (Oxford: Oxford University Press, 2001), p. 239.

4 Torbjörn Tännsjö, 'The secular model of the multi-cultural state', *Inquiry* (1995), 38: 109–17.

5 As was stressed in Chapter 3, D. Miller, *Citizenship and National Identity*, has elaborated on (and, indeed, overstated) this point.

6 I owe the term 'democratic determinism' to Michèle Micheletti who mistakenly accused me of having used it when I gave a talk on global democracy at the department of political science at Stockholm University. I did not use it but I now think I *should* have done so.

7 I have this quotation from Derek Heater, *World Citizenship and World Government* (London: Macmillan, 1996), p. 189.

8 Heater, *World Citizenship*.

9 D. Zolo, *Cosmopolis. Prospects for World Government* (Cambridge: Polity Press, 1997), pp. 137–8.

10 Melchior, Telle and Wiig, *Globalisation and Inequality*, pp. 116–17, 21.

11 The first author who introduced this idea seems to have been James Lorimer, in *The Application of the Principle of Relative or Proportional Equality to International Organisations* (1877). I have this from F. H. Hinsley. According

to Hinsley, Lorimer 'prided himself on being the first to suggest that the national and the international fields should be rigidly separated and that the sphere of the international government should be rigidly confined to the latter' (*Power and the Pursuit of Peace*, p. 136).

12 In my radicalism I seem to be in agreement with some of my philosopher colleagues, however, such as A. C. Ewing, who expressed his hope that 'the United Nations Organisation will gradually, by explicit amendment or tacitly in the course of its working, come nearer to a federation', *The Individual, the State, and World Government*, p. 315 and with Kai Nielsen who, in 'World government, security and social justice', in S. Luper-Foy (ed.), *Problems of International Justice* (Boulder, CO: Westview Press, 1998) argued that we need world government as a 'Leviathan' to grant us peace.

13 Cf., for example, the influential Montreux Declaration of the World Movement for World Federal Government, issued in 1947 (second paragraph).

14 D. Archibugi, 'Principles of cosmopolitan democracy', in D. Archibugi, D. Held and M. Köhler (eds), *Re-imagining Political Community: Studies in Cosmopolitan Democracy* (London: Polity, 1998), p. 209.

15 Held, *Democracy and the Global Order*, p. 236.

16 I have the quotation from Derek Heater, *World Citizenship and Government*, p. 163.

17 Rousseau, *The Social Contract*, book II, chapter 2.

18 See Kelsen, *Peace Through Law*, pp. 5–6, and Rawls, *The Law of Peoples*, p. 36.

19 Kant, *Perpetual Peace*, p. 259.

Conclusion

1 See Chapter 1.

Bibliography

Acemoglu, D. and Robinson, J., *Economic Origins of Dictatorship and Democracy* (Cambridge: Cambridge University Press, 2006).

Adams, J., 'Letter to John Penn', *Works* (Boston, 1852 and 1865), IV, 205.

Appiah, K. A., *Cosmopolitanism: Ethics in a World of Strangers* (New York: Norton, 2006).

Archibugi, D., 'Principles of cosmopolitan democracy', in D. Archibugi, D. Held and M. Köhler (eds), *Re-imagining Political Community: Studies in Cosmopolitan Democracy* (London: Polity, 1998).

Arizona Water Resource, Nov.–Dec. 1999, Vol. 8, No. 3.

Armaments, Disarmament and National Security: SIPRI Yearbook 2007 (Stockholm: Stockholm International Peace Research Institute, 2007).

Arrow, K. J., *Social Choice and Individual Values* (New York: Wiley, 1951).

Barry, B., 'Statism and nationalism: a cosmopolitan critique', in Ian Shapiro and Lea Brilmayer (eds), *Global Justice* (New York: New York University Press, 1999), pp. 12–66.

Beetham, D., *Democracy: A Beginner's Guide* (Oxford: Oneworld, 2005).

Beitz, C. R., *Political Theory and International Relations* (Princeton, NJ: Princeton University Press, 1979).

Bentham, J., *A Plan for a Universal and Perpetual Peace*, http://www.la.utexas.edu/research/poltheory/bentham/pil/pil.e04.html, accessed 10 November 2005.

Bergström, L., 'Democracy and political boundaries', in Folke Tersman (ed.), *The Viability and Desirability of Global Democracy*, Stockholm Studies in Democratic Theory, Vol. III (Stockholm: Stockholm University, 2007).

Bickel, A., *The Least Dangerous Branch* (Indianapolis, IN: Bobbs-Merrill, 1962).

Black, D., 'On the rationale of group decision-making', *Journal of Political Economy* (1948), 56: 23–34.

Brighouse, H. and Fleurbaey, M., 'On the fair allocation of power' (Mimeo, 2005).

Bull, H., *The Anarchial Society* (London: Macmillan, 1977).

Burnheim, J., *Is Democracy Possible?* (Cambridge: Polity Press, 1985).

Cloots, Anacharsis, *La République universelle* (1792).

Crucé, E., *Noveau Cynée* (1623–4).

145

Dahl, R. A., 'Decision-making in a democracy: the supreme court as a national policy-maker', *Journal of Public Law* (1957), 6: 279–95.

Dahl, R. A., *Polyarchy: Participation and Opposition* (New Haven, CT: Yale University Press, 1971).

Dower, N., *An Introduction to Global Citizenship* (Edinburgh: Edinburgh University Press, 2003).

Dryzek, J. S., *Deliberative Democracy and Beyond. Liberals, Critics, Contestations* (Oxford: Oxford University Press, 2000).

Dwyer, J., 'Global health justice', *Bioethics* (2005), 19: 460–75.

Eley, J. H., *Democracy and Distrust – A Theory of Judicial Review* (Cambridge, MA: Harvard University Press, 1980).

Ewing, A. C., *The Individual, the State, and World Government* (New York: Macmillan, 1947).

Faeron, J. D. and Laitin, D. D., 'Ethnicity, insurgency, and civil war', *American Political Science Review* (2003), 97: 75–90.

Falk, R. and Strauss, A., 'On the creation of a global peoples' assembly: legitimacy and the power of popular sovereignty', *Stanford Journal of International Law* (2000) 36: 191–220.

Fishkin, J. S., *The Voice of the People: Public Opinion and Democracy* (New Haven, CT: Yale University Press, 1995).

Frank, A. G., *Dependent Accumulation and Underdevelopment* (New York: Monthly Review Press, 1979).

Galtung, J., 'Alternative models for global democracy', in Barry Holden (ed.), *Global Democracy. Key Debates* (London: Routledge, 2000).

Glover, J., *Humanity: A Moral History of the Twentieth Century* (London: Jonathan Cape, 1999).

Griffin, N., *The Selected Letters of Bertrand Russell: The Public Years, 1914–1970* (London: Routledge, 1992).

Hardin, G., 'The tragedy of the commons', *Science* (1968) 162: 1243–8.

Hart, H. L. A., *The Concept of Law*, 2nd edn with postscript by J. Raz and P. Bulloch (eds) (Oxford: Oxford University Press, 1994).

Heater, D., *World Citizenship and Government* (London: Macmillan, 1996).

Hegre, T., Gates, S., Gleditsch, N. P. and Ellingson, T., 'Toward a democratic civil peace?', *American Political Science Review* (2001) 95: 33–48.

Held, D., *Democracy and the Global Order: From the Modern State to Cosmopolitan Governance* (Cambridge: Polity Press, 1995).

Held, D., *The Global Covenant: The Social Democratic Alternative to the Washington Consensus* (Cambridge: Polity Press, 2004).

Hinsley, F. H., *Power and the Pursuit of Peace: Theory and Practice in the History of Relations Between States* (Cambridge: Cambridge University Press, 1963).

Hobbes, T., *Leviathan* [1651] here quoted from, J. C. A. Gaskin (ed.), Thomas

Bibliography

Hobbes, *Leviathan* (Oxford: Oxford University Press, 1996).

Human Security Report (Oxford: Oxford University Press, 2005).

Kant, I., *Perpetual Peace*, here quoted from Ted Humphrey (transl.), *Perpetual Peace and other Essays on Politics, History, and Morals* (Indianapolis, IN: Hacket, 1983).

Kelsen, H., *Peace Through Law* (Chapel Hill, NC: University of North Carolina Press, 1944).

Kymlicka, W., *Politics in the Vernacular: Nationalism, Multiculturalism, and Citizenship* (Oxford: Oxford University Press, 2001).

Locke, J., *Second Treatise of Government*. Many editions exist. Quoted here from a critical edition with an introduction and *apparatus criticus* by Peter Laslett (Cambridge: Cambridge University Press, 1960).

Lorimer, J., *The Application of the Principle of Relative or Proportional Equality to International Organisations* (1877).

MacIntyre, A., *Whose Justice? Which Rationality?* (Notre Dame, IN: University of Notre Dame Press, 1991).

Madison, J., *The Federalist Papers* (New York: Doubleday, 1966).

McNally, D., *Another World Is Possible. Globalization and Anti-Capitalism* (Winnipeg, Manitoba: Arbeiter Ring, 2002).

Melchior, A., Telle, K. and Wiig, H., *Globalisation and Inequality: World Income Distribution and Living Standards, 1960–1998*, Oslo: Royal Norwegian Ministry of Foreign Affairs; Norwegian Institute of International Affairs, 2000 (Report No. 6B) (full text at: http://odin.dep.no/ud).

Miller, D., *Citizenship and National Identity* (Cambridge: Polity Press, 2000).

Moore, J. N., Editorial comments: 'Solving the war puzzle', *American Journal of International Law* (2003), 97(2): 282, 284.

Muller, E. N. and Weede, E., 'Cross-national variations in political violence: A rational action approach', *Journal of Conflict Resolution* (1990), 34: 624–51.

Naess, A., *Ecology, Community and Lifestyle: Outline of an Ecosophy* (Cambridge: Cambridge University Press, 1989).

Nielsen, K., 'World government, security and social justice', in S. Luper-Foy (ed.), *Problems of International Justice* (Boulder, CO: Westview Press, 1988).

Nielsen, K., *Globalization and Justice* (Amherst, NY: Humanity Books, 2003).

Nozick, R., *Anarchy, State, and Utopia* (Oxford: Blackwell, 1974).

Pitkin, H. F., *The Concept of Representation* (Berkeley, CA: University of California Press, 1967).

Pogge, T. W., 'Cosmopolitanism and sovereignty', *Ethics* (1992), 103: 48–75.

Pogge, T. W., 'An egalitarian law of peoples', *Philosophy and Public Affairs* (1994), 23: 195–224.

Pogge, T. W., *World Poverty and Human Rights: Cosmopolitan Responsibilities and Reforms* (Cambridge: Polity Press, 2002).

Rabinowicz, W. and Bovens, L., 'Democratic answers to complex questions – an epistemic perspective', in M. Sintonen (ed.), *Socratic Method of Questioning as Philosophy and as Method* (Dordrecht: Kluwer, 2004).

Rawls, J., *A Theory of Justice* (Cambridge, MA: Harvard University Press, 1971).

Rawls, J., *The Law of Peoples* (Cambridge, MA: Harvard University Press, 1999).

Riker, W., *Liberalism Against Populism: A Confrontation Between the Theory of Democracy and the Theory of Social Choice* (San Francisco, CA: Freeman, 1982).

Rousseau, J.-J., *The Social Contract* (Harmondsworth: Penguin, 1968).

Rummel, R. J., *Power Kills: Democracy as a Method of Nonviolence* (New Brunswick, NJ: Transaction, 1997).

Rummel, R. J., 'Interview', *Peace Magazine*, May–June 1999, p. 10, available at: http://www.peacemagazine.org/archive/v15n3p10.htm.

Sandel, M., *Liberalism and the Limits of Justice*, 2nd edn (Cambridge: Cambridge University Press, 1998).

Schumpeter. J., *Capitalism, Socialism, and Democracy* (London: Unwin, 1943).

Schweickart, D., *After Capitalism* (Lanham, MD: Rowman and Littlefield, 2002).

Singer, P., 'Famine, affluence, and morality', *Philosophy and Public Affairs* (1972) 1: 229–43.

Singer, P., *One World. The Ethics of Globalization* (New Haven, CT: Yale University Press, 2002).

Smith, N., *The Endgame of Globalization* (New York: Routledge, 2005).

Steiner, H., 'Just taxation and international redistribution', in Ian Shapiro and Lea Brilmayer (eds), *Global Justice* (New York: New York University Press, 1999).

Sunstein, C. R., *Republic.com* (Princeton, NJ: Princeton University Press, 2001).

Svedberg, P., 'World income distribution: which way?', *Journal of Development Studies* (2004), 40(5): 1–32.

Tännsjö, T., *Populist Democracy. A Defence* (London: Routledge, 1992).

Tännsjö, T., 'The secular model of the multi-cultural state', *Inquiry* (1995) 38: 109–17.

Tännsjö, T., *Hedonistic Utilitarianism* (Edinburgh: Edinburgh University Press, 1998).

Tännsjö, T., *Du skall understundom dräpa!* (*Thou Shalt Sometimes Kill!*) (Stockholm: Prisma, 2001) (the book exists also in German and Norwegian translations, but not, yet, in English).

Tännsjö, T., 'Rational injustice', *Philosophy of the Social Sciences* (2006) 36: 423–39.

Taylor, C., 'Conditions of an unforced consensus on human rights', in J. R. Bauer and D. Bell (eds), *The East Asian Challenge for Human Rights* (New York: Cambridge University Press, 1999).

Unger, P., *Living High and Letting Die. Our Illusion of Innocence* (Oxford: Oxford University Press, 1996).

Bibliography

Walzer, M., *Thick and Thin* (Notre Dame, IN: University of Notre Dame Press, 1994).

Wells, H. G., *Anticipations* (London: Chapman & Hall, 1901).

Wells, H. G., *Imperialism and the Open Conspiracy* (London: Faber & Faber, 1929).

Wells, H. G., *The Common Sense of War and Peace* (Harmondsworth: Penguin, 1940).

Zolo, D., *Cosmopolis: Prospects for World Government* (Cambridge: Polity Press, 1997).

Index

Index

deliberative democracy, 76–8
'Democracy Unbound', vii
democratic determinism, 119, 143n6
Derrida, Jacques, xii, 106, 142n13
desalination, 63
despotism, 127, 128
dictatorship, 72
'difference principle', 41, 42–3
Dimdins, Girt, vii
disease, 55
distributive justice, 30–1

economic development, 120–2
economic growth, 36
economic sanctions, 66
economy, lack of world, 7
egalitarianism, 32–7
elitism, 75–6, 84–8
endangered species, 53, 64–6
English language, 120
environment, 9, 53–67
epistemic model, 79–80, 81–2
equilibrium, 48
European Convention on Human
    Rights, 94
European Parliament, 113
European Union, xi, 106, 119, 125, 126
Ewing, A. C., ix, 96, 101, 144n12
exports, 50

farming, subsidies to, 50
federation, 2, 3, 127
Finland, 20, 87
fishing, 64, 65
France, 21
free trade, 40, 50–1
fundamentalism, religious, 129–30

Galtung, Johan, 98, 99, 115, 142n2
Germany, 20, 86
    attitudes to military, 100, 101
global high court *see* high court
global justice, 2, 30–52

Global Peoples' Assembly *see*
    Peoples' Assembly
global resources tax, 43–6, 49
global warming, 2, 9, 53, 54–9, 89,
    128, 134
globalisation, x, 92, 130
Glover, Jonathan, 16–17
'Go', 102
Goodin, Bob, vii
Gould, Carol, vii
Grant, Ulysses S., 50–1
greenhouse gases *see* CO_2 emissions
Grenada, 21
Guatemala, 23

Habermas, Jürgen, xii, 106, 142n13
Hart, H. L. A., 40
Harvard Middle East Water Project,
    63
Held, David, 74, 124
Helsinki Declaration, 94
high court, 99, 115
House of Lords of United Nations,
    96, 97, 99
Human Security Report, 16, 17, 18, 24,
    26

India, 96–7
    attitudes to military, 101–2, 104
    economy, 102–3
    global warming, 56–7
Indochina, 21
Indonesia, 23
interests, aggregation of, 79, 80–1,
    83, 84
Intergovernmental Panel on Climate
    Change (IPCC), 54, 55
International Court of Justice and
    Equality through Law, 23, 94
International Criminal Court, 94
International Monetary Fund (IMF),
    94
internet, 77

151

Index

Rawls, John, 2, 41–2, 118
redistribution, 49–50
Reinfeldt, Fredrik, 57
religious fundamentalism, 129–30
representative democracy, 72–4
republicanism, 3, 12–14, 19
Riker, William, 140–1n1(ch5)
Roman Empire, 11
Rousseau, Jean-Jacques, 2, 126, 133
Rummel, Rudy, 19–20, 21–2, 89
Russell, Bertrand, 11, 137n2(ch2)

sanctions, 88, 125–6
    economic, 66
Scandinavia, 49–50, 107–8
Schumpeter, Joseph, 75–6, 85–6
Schweickart, David, 47, 122
sea grass beds, 64, 65
Security Council, 112
Singer, Peter, 49, 55, 56–7
socialism, 9, 46–8, 52, 122
Soros, George, 108
South Africa, 23, 88
sovereignty, 133–4
    shared, 122–6, 139n13
Soviet Union, 12, 47, 104
Spain, 87, 107
Stability Pact, 126
state-market system, Chinese, 47
Stern report, 59
subsidiarity, 124–5
subsidies to farming, 50
Suez War, 20
superpowers, xi–xii, 6, 12, 18–19, 68, 92
Svedberg, Peter, 34–6, 102–3
Sweden
    attitudes to military, 100, 101
    global warming, 57, 58–9
Swedish Research Council, vii
Switzerland, 87

taxes, 43–6, 118, 135

terrorism, 28, 127; *see also* anti-terrorism
Tersman, Folke, vii
Thailand, 23
Thorseth, May, vii
Tokyo War Crimes Tribunal Charter, 94
tragedy of the commons, 59, 65, 89, 128, 133
twentieth century, violence of, 16–17

Unger, Peter, 49
United Nations, x, xi, 18, 26–7, 96–9, 134
United Nations Charter on Human Rights, 94
United Nations Human Rights Council, 130
United States, 23, 87, 91, 94–5, 98, 101, 113, 115
    civil rights movement, 88
    global warming, 56–9
    military resources, 104–5, 127–8, 135
    political apathy, 85
    superpower, xii, 6, 12, 92
    wars, 21, 22, 61, 89, 113
utilitarianism, 31–2, 46–8

Venezuela, 23
Vietnam War, 21, 22

wars, 10, 14, 132, 133; *see also* peace
    civil, 24, 25, 28
    Cold, 21, 24
    Iraq, second, 61, 89, 113
    number of, 16, 17, 18, 24
    participants in, 19–23
    Suez, 20
    Vietnam, 21, 22
water resources, 53, 62–4
Weadon, Donald, 102
wei ch'i, 102

Wells, H. G., ix, 4, 68, 137n2 (ch1)
whales, 66
World Bank, 94
World Federalist Movement (WFM),
    x–xi
world government, 1–7, 97–8, 113–
    14
World Movement for World Federal
    Government, 123

world parliament, 1, 83, 84, 95,
    113–14, 135; *see also* People's
    Assembly
World Trade Organization (WTO), 94

Yugoslavia, former, 25

Zetterquist, Ola, vii
Zolo, Danilo, 120–1